To everybody

IF TEACHERS WERE FREE

BY
RICHARD RENFIELD

Foreword by ELIZABETH DUNCAN KOONTZ

038396

PUBLISHED BY ACROPOLIS BOOKS/WASHINGTON, D.C. 20009

The author gratefully acknowledges the permission granted by

• NEA Publications Division to use the photos in this book, taken by Joe DiDio and Carl Purcell;

• Mrs. Susan Epperson, a former teacher in Little Rock, to use her statement challenging the anti-evolution law in Arkansas (p. 19);

• The National Education Association and the American Association of School Administrators to refer to the seven values of the spirit of science (pp. 20, 28, 139);

• John Wiley and Sons, Inc., to quote Christian Bay (p. 27);

• Professor E. Paul Torrance of the University of Georgia to use his definition of creativity (p. 28);

• the McGraw-Hill Book Company to quote Richard Armour (p. 44);

• Sam Shepard, Assistant Superintendent of Schools in St. Louis, Missouri, to tell his tale about expectations (p. 89);

• the National Association of Secondary School Principals to refer to its *Curriculum Report* (p. 89);

• the National Committee for Support of the Public Schools to quote John Holt (p. 127);

• Professor Charles Frankel of Columbia University to paraphrase his admonition about our wits (p. 141);

• Space Publications, Inc., to use its quotation of former Air Force Secretary Harold Brown (p. 143);

• John Poppy, Senior Editor of *Look* Magazine, to quote him and George B. Leonard (p. 149);

• PDK Publications to reproduce the excerpt in *Phi Delta Kappan* from a *New York Sun* editorial of 1902 (p. 154).

© Second Revised Edition, Copyright 1972 by Richard Renfield, Ph.D.

© Copyright 1969 by Richard Renfield, Ph.D.

First Printing: March, 1969

ACROPOLIS BOOKS
Colortone Building, 2400 17th St., N.W.
Washington, D. C. 20009

Printed in the United States of America by
COLORTONE CREATIVE PRINTING,
Washington, D. C. 20009

Type set in Baskerville and Caledonia
with Ultima headings
by Colortone Typographic Division, Inc.

Design by Design and Art Studio 2400, Inc.

LIBRARY OF CONGRESS CATALOG NUMBER 77-80095 / SBN: 87491-005-6

Foreword

Anyone whose mind is closed to educational—and social—change or who fears his own lack of competence to cope with change should not read this book!

For in spite of himself, he will find himself in agreement with this exceptionally incisive, logical discourse—sans pedagese—on the status, needs, and rationale for improvement of American education.

Seldom does one find such precise, well-defined criticism followed by so realistic an approach to what should be.

The author presents a dynamic case for a new, highly demanding, total collaboration among those involved in the education enterprise—from beginning to end.

He has given meaning and life to the term "relevancy," leading the reader toward a striking perception of the future and of education's role in that future. His "anti-prediction" captivates the reader.

The author has translated the ofttimes unspoken frustrations of middle class parents and students. He has movingly articulated the loudly-voiced discontent of ghetto and non-white parents and students. He offers a means by which productive order can be brought out of confusion and chaos.

Dr. Renfield has presented to all educators a challenge that dares them (1) to pursue academic freedom, and (2) to accept responsibility for demonstrating that their planning, teaching, methodology and purposes have actually led to the development of pupils' rational capacities. This challenge is all the more urgent when one attempts to describe life 20 or 50 years hence and realizes the tremendous change that has occurred during the past decade or two. It is simply no longer reasonable to prescribe educational content in terms of courses, credit hours, grades, or books.

The author's analyses hold great import also for institutions now plagued by student unrest. Student demands for recognition and for a curriculum related to life are ofttimes dramatic outgrowths of a sense that they are not being prepared to cope with tomorrow—or even today—or to make the world a better place. Dr. Renfield does not specify these problems, yet his book is decidedly relevant to them.

For educators, boards of education, and the public in general, this book is a must if they truly and honestly desire to make American education meaningful for the millions who live in this land of advanced science and technology among the peoples of an ever-shrinking world.

—Elizabeth Duncan Koontz *

* *Mrs. Koontz is now Director of the Woman's Bureau of the Department of Labor; she was the first Negro to be elected President of the National Education Association (July 1968- January 1969).*

Contents

PREFACE   **9**

I .... **IN THE BEGINNING**   **11**
The Great Debate   13
Virtual Violence Over Values   19
A School is Born   27
A Shocking Proposal   32
Mr. Chubb's Luck Persists   35
Puberty Rites   37

II .... **THE ESSENCE OF THE SYSTEM**   **41**
Can We Rely on Pupils' Interests?   44
Fear of Chaos and Imbalance   50
Planning by Teachers   58
Pupil Grouping   62
Pupil Evaluation   66
A Merit System that Probably Rewards Merit   70

III .... **FROM SEX TO STATUS**   **74**
Sex   76
College Admission Requirements   79
The Teachers' Time Problem   84
Can Incompetent Teachers be Trusted with
So Much Discretion?   86
A New Vision of Teaching   88
Teacher Status   92
Potseloo and The Disadvantaged   95

IV .... **IN THE GHETTO**   **103**
. . . And He Became a Little Child   104
The Pediatrician and the Schools   107
An Idea   112
Beauty and the Bug   116
Theory Meets Practice   119
Rays of Sunshine   124

V .... **ALL ABOUT THE FUTURE**   **127**
Yesterday and Tomorrow   131
In Praise of Public Schools   144
But . . .   149
A Plea for Ignorance?   154

Preface

PARABLE

An emissary of God came to earth.

And he visited a school.

And he said, "Why do you despise your young?"

And he was told, "But we love them. We do for
them what we know to be best for them."

And he replied, "You do not rely on their own
motivations."

And he was told, "But their own motivations will
not take them where they need to go."

And he said, "Why do you despise your young?"

      *   *   *

Asked the child of her father, "Tell me, how should
life be?"

And he said, "That's a question that's way
beyond me."

She objected, "It can't be, 'cause you're a grown
man,

You can answer my question, I know that you can."

"My mind's full of facts, and of mem'ries, and
feeling,

But your question wants wisdom, and you are
    appealing
for the essence of all that I've learned in my days,
and for power to dream, and to think, and appraise."
"But to be an adult, I thought that it meant
to think deeply and wisely, or to have that intent."
The father sat quiet, then breathed the suggestion,
"I really suspect that you've answered your
    question."

(continued later)

POEM

Woman to Samuel Johnson: *"Mr. Smith, I believe."*
Samuel Johnson to woman: *"If you believe that, you'll
believe anything."*

PROPHECY

*Education is deep in the dark ages. It has to be, for
our knowledge of the human mind is miniscule. We do not
know what a thought is. We do not know the difference
within the human mind (whatever that is) between knowing
that Columbus (or was it someone else?) discovered America
for the European world and knowing how to recognize blue.
We do not know the difference between a brain that has
learned French and a brain that has not, or between a brain
that thinks poorly and a brain that thinks well. We see
the results of intelligence, but we do not know what it is.
In short, we are ignorant of the very stuff of education.*

*As a result, education, even at its very best, is an in-
efficient enterprise. Over the millenia in which men have
been teaching their children, they have developed a few*

9

methods of teaching and even a few theories on how to do the job. But basically learning remains a matter of "practice-makes-perfect," with various incentives and pressures thrown in, if necessary, to stimulate practice, and with much missing as well as hitting. We cannot conceive of learning to talk, sew, play ball, or read as anything other than a matter of long practice, some of it probably barren of any contribution and even damaging to the learner's motivation. We cannot imagine learning history or Russian or bridge except through a period of apprenticeship.

Some day we may learn what a thought is, what knowledge is, what learning is, or what intelligence is. We may be able to specify the physiological or chemical or electrical reality of knowing a given fact, thinking a given thought, recognizing blue as opposed to red, or being intelligent. On that day, the foundations of education, as we have known it, will crumble. And the education we know today, for all the wonders and horrors it has enabled men to perform, will be seen as a most primitive operation. Only the coming of language was an educational revolution of remotely comparable power.

Given this background of ignorance, I can hardly claim that the pages of this small book will reveal the ultimate in educational wisdom. I can claim only that they contain conclusions based on some years of acquaintance with educational philosophy and practice. In this dark age, what less poor justification can anyone claim for imposing on readers his views of what education ought to be?

Our path starts in a once-tranquil suburb, passes through a turbulent ghetto, and concludes, immodestly enough, with an analysis of the future and of the needs of education.

—R. R.

10

CHAPTER I

In the beginning

Tradition has it that Potseloo, an area of fertile farmland, was first settled by a family of Russian Cossack immigrants to the United States. The father, whose romantic soul was moved by the similarity between the black soil here and in his native Ukraine, is reputed to have knelt down and kissed it. He thereupon chose his homestead, calling it Potseluy (Russian for kiss). Gradually, the area came to be called Potseloo.*

For decades Potseloo was little more than a

---

* Accented on the first syllable, like Waterloo. The middle syllable, "se," rhymes with the usual pronunciation of "the." Any map showing Potseloo is to be admired for the imagination and creativity which characterized its preparation.

few dispersed farm houses. Then, after World War II, the suburban sprawl from the city of Letlit began to encroach on Potseloo's farmland.

Potseloo's school board had once operated a one-room school of its own. Later, it contracted for the use of an elementary school and a high school in Letlit. As Potseloo grew, the board began to weigh the possibility of reestablishing a school system of its own. The question was solely *whether* to establish schools. The type of education they would supply was not at first debated. They would be carbon copies, on a small scale, of the schools in Letlit.

THE GREAT DEBATE

As Potseloo pondered its problem, Orville Chubb, a 35-year-old sixth-grade teacher from Letlit and resident of Potseloo, appeared before the board to expound his bizarre views on education. They were bizarre not because they were original (which they were not) but because he took them seriously. Were it not for his tireless reiteration of these views, Potseloo today would probably have an ordinary school and would not enjoy its world renown.

In his eleven years of public-school teaching, Mr. Chubb had become convinced that schools were over-organized. The restraints and requirements they placed on teachers were, he felt, incompatible with excellence in teaching. Some of the fault lay with administrators. Mr. Chubb had spent several months as an instructor of military etiquette during his two-year Army career. There, he contended, his superiors had given him such detailed directions that he was more a puppet dangling from a string than a human being supporting a head. But he could cite some administrative transgressions from his career at Letlit, too. He recalled with particular feeling the repeated warnings of one principal to enthusiastic beginning teachers: "We don't do things that way in this school!"

The most pervasive restraints, however, related to the content of the curriculum. Mr. Chubb quoted author-educators John C. Holt and Edgar Z. Friedenberg in support of his view that school curriculums often prevent learning or insure that it will be mediocre. How, he asked, can a curriculum be the right one for most pupils, or even for any pupils, if it is planned by persons who are not in moment-to-moment contact with each pupil who will be subjected to it? "Can we honestly believe," he continued, "that the time of all 30 children in a class is best used by sitting them all down from 10 to 11 o'clock every Monday through Friday morning and having them learn history? Even if we let each of them study a different facet of history, or let each go through the material at his own speed, it would be an incredible coincidence if the best thing for all of them is really to spend that time on history."

For decades educators had recognized the importance of motivation in learning. Mr. Chubb maintained that motivation was becoming more crucial with each passing year. He cited two reasons.

The first was the prediction, which he shared with Glenn T. Seaborg, Chairman of the Atomic Energy Commission, that virtually all the tasks by which Americans now earn a living will soon be better performed by machines and computers. Almost all of life will then consist of what has traditionally been considered leisure time. The only inexhaustible occupations of man will be the pursuit of knowledge and understanding and the effort to relate them to one's attitudes and actions. In such a world, the intellectually indolent will find idleness and perhaps create mischief. But for the prepared—for those who love to learn—life will be a perpetual opportunity to grow and, through understanding, to develop a closer relationship with the universe.

The second reason for an increasing emphasis on motivation lay in the changing nature of knowledge. Mr. Chubb was less concerned than many progressive education theorists with relating learning to pupils' ordinary experience. That concern, he argued, was progressive in the past; it was of declining relevance to the future in which today's young people would be adults. He predicted that a growing proportion of learning would have to be, in a sense, second-hand. Increasingly, the knowledge of mankind is not something the individual sees, touches, or experiences in his social relations. Much of man's search for reality is removing him from the realm of gross experience. Yet second-hand learning can be real and attractive to pupils. If it grows from one's own interests, it can satisfy one's genuine desire to be acquainted with the world. It becomes just as real to a person, just as much a part of his life, as what he sees and touches. To use Swiss child psychologist Jean Piaget's language, the pupil assimilates the knowledge, fitting it into his mind-set, and accommodates his mind-set to each new learning. He becomes capable of surpassing, rather than merely repeating, the accomplishments of man to date.

If the school was to nurture love of learning into a life-long force, Mr. Chubb contended, the school board must refrain from specifying the content of learning. It should state the goals of education in broad terms and then leave teachers free to pursue those goals. In no case should a subject be named.

A number of teacher educators and young teachers from Letlit supported Mr. Chubb. A surprising number of Potselovians* were also willing to give his ideas a try. But opposition was intense. Many adults were unalterably convinced that an institution without pre-planned activities and without pre-planned doses of knowledge to administer was not a school at all. Most agreed that education should pursue many goals in addition to the transmission of knowledge and should take account of individual differences. But a system which required no specific subjects and which based itself totally on individual interests was beyond their ken. A few even hinted that it might be subversive.

Some experienced educators from Letlit contended that the Chubb plan—or non-plan—was insane. They held that, without a curriculum planned in at least its broad outlines, and without certain requirements for all pupils, most pupils would not

---

* Mistakenly referred to in some countries as Potselooloos.

learn many of the things they needed to know. Their long experience, they maintained, permitted no other conclusion.

Mr. Chubb countered that experience can blind as well as enrich. It can delude one into identifying the possible with the experienced. "Children are so curious about the world," he said. "If we would respond to their curiosity, rather than tell them what we want them to be curious about, they would learn far more than our best teachers today can teach them. We would be cooperating with nature rather than fighting it."

Mr. Chubb realized that some students, left totally to their own devices, would choose to learn about matters that would prove of little use to them; a few might choose to spend days on end learning nothing at all—which, as anyone knows, is the right of adults alone. But the Chubb plan did not call for leaving students totally to their own devices; learning activities would be worked out in close consultation between the pupil and his teacher or teachers.

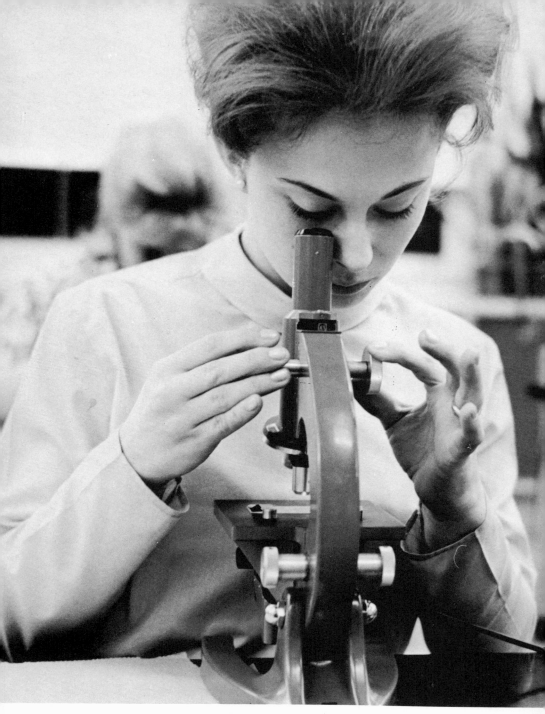

WE DO NOT KNOW THE DIFFERENCE BETWEEN A BRAIN THAT
HAS LEARNED BIOLOGY AND A BRAIN THAT HAS NOT . . .

VIRTUAL VIOLENCE OVER VALUES

"In place of a rational system of knowledge, men erected fantastic and pretentious edifices of misinformation concerning themselves and the world around them. Within these walls of their own building they systematically imprisoned themselves, shackling themselves to them with bonds of emotion and social compulsion. Inside the enclosures, moreover, they put on a kind of puppet show. In this the leading roles were played by imagined spirits, both petty and grandiose, and the main operations consisted of magic events on every conceivable scale."—Hermann Muller, late Professor of Zoology at Indiana University, Nobel Laureate 1946; from a 1958 Speech.

"To what extent can a state government . . . suppress the search for knowledge, for truth?"—Mrs. Susan Epperson, former high school teacher in Little Rock, challenging the anti-evolution law in Arkansas, December 1965.

The question of whether individual subjects should be specified was debated with some warmth. The question of the basic goals of education aroused still greater passion. On this matter even Mr. Chubb, who had gained a reputation for equanimity and tact, once lost his temper. The incident was quickly dubbed "Chubb's flub."

19

Mr. Chubb favored the seven values of the spirit of science* as the goals of education. Six of these values were quickly accepted as legitimate and even obvious goals of education. But the second value, "questioning of all things," aroused a storm of dissension, swirling basically around the question: "Is an American a doubter or a believer?"

Some Potselovians argued that the questioning of all things might threaten patriotism, God, sexual morality, and something they called "the social fabric." They proposed that inculcation of the ideals of "the American way of life" be among the basic goals of education. In particular, they wanted children to learn love of country, hatred of communism, devotion to free enterprise, and recognition of the evils of alcohol, tobacco, and drugs.

Others argued that a person who questions all things was a safe person. Could a person who questions, they asked rhetorically, come to favor a form of government, such as communism, in which the questioning of all things is forbidden? Could he lightly take up smoking or drug addiction? If he finds fault with his country or its institutions, is that unpatriotic? The doubter, they argued, eventually arrives at certain beliefs, and these beliefs need not be feared.

It was clear from the start that the majority was on the side of the questioners, but the believers

---

*See National Education Association and American Association of School Administrators, Educational Policies Commission, *Education and the Spirit of Science.* Washington, D. C.: The Commission, 1966. p. 15. See also pp. 28 and 139 of *If Teachers Were Free.*

were vocal and had some embarrassing questions of their own. Weren't their opponents, in assuming that the right answers would automatically flow from an objective questioning of all things, merely insisting on the right conclusions without being honest enough to admit it? Indeed, isn't the value of questioning all things, like the other values of the spirit of science, itself a preference which the self-styled questioners would force on all pupils?

The questioners replied by insisting on their willingness to let everyone draw his own conclusions; they were ready to countenance the possibility that some might conclude "wrong." Moreover, they feared that insistence, even if subtle, on the proper conclusions often boomerangs. Some students, discerning a hesitation to permit free thought about certain issues, merely have their appetites whetted to taste of forbidden fruit and even to conclude "wrong."

What of the charge that the majority was intent upon inculcating in pupils the values of the spirit of science? The usual reply was that these values are the very antithesis of inculcation. If one truly learns to question all things, mustn't he question the value and consequences of questioning all things as well? Mustn't he decide for himself whether uncertainty is an appropriate way of life, and what alternatives there are? Isn't the essence of the spirit of science a request to each person that he be himself, rather than submitting without thought or consciousness to the influences of his environment, like a vegetable? This is the unique virtue of the values of the spirit of science: that they alone can be taught without inculcation, that is, with full respect for the dignity of the individual. Or so the questioners argued.

One evening, after a speech to a men's club, Mr. Chubb was asked how he could justify his apparent desire to place little children in an atmosphere of insecurity and doubt. His reaction was startling. "It seems to me," he began, "that you don't honestly believe in freedom. You don't really want it for your children. Are you afraid of freedom? Do you feel safe only when certain areas of the mind are enslaved? Apparently you think you have found some definitive answers? Should we force our children to agree?"

Heedless of the astonishment he had provoked, Mr. Chubb proceeded to compound his flub. "When an American traveler criticizes the lack of free press in the Soviet Union, Russians often answer, 'If our Party knows the truth, why should it present other sides in the newspapers and confuse the people?' What strikes me is how many Americans think just like these Russians!"

Contempt was unkind; to equate a pillar of the community with communists was unforgivable. Interrupting the embarrassed silence, the questioner generously suggested that his question had been worded unclearly; it was intended to reflect, not dogmatism, but a sincere concern for little children. Mr. Chubb, acknowledging the magnanimity of the effort to attribute the blame to the question, quickly apologized. But the damage was done. Some citizens were more convinced than ever that, at bottom, Mr.

Chubb was as dogmatic as those he accused of dogmatism. The strain produced by strenuous months of promoting his cause, they chortled, had finally laid bare his true nature.

Potseloo had a weekly newspaper, the *Potseloo American,* dedicated largely to advertisements and to reports of births, marriages, deaths, and Little League baseball results. Reporting of the education debate was sketchy at best. One issue, however, carried an open letter from a group of teachers to the Potseloo school board. The letter bore the bizarre title, "Is Freedom of Inquiry American?" It provoked considerable discussion, and much indignation among citizens who read no further than the title. Since the writers were teachers, it impressed the school board. I therefore cite it in full:

"In the United States, the goals of education are for the most part determined by the representatives of the people at the local and the state levels. It is fitting that those who pay the piper call the tune. It is fitting, but it also creates grave problems. Among them is the fact that the goals may be mutually contradictory.

"It is common for school boards to include among the goals of education both the ability to think and patriotism. These goals are perfectly compatible—provided that patriotism is not defined as an emotional identification of the United States with goodness and justice. Unfortunately, many communities define it just that way. They do not commit the definition to writing, but they unmistakably clarify their intent if a teacher permits his class to draw

23

some seriously negative conclusions about the American way of life.

"If a community must specify patriotism as a goal, let patriotism be understood as a desire to help the United States become a better society by the fruits of one's most critical thinking. The ability to think is consistent with that definition of patriotism. If a community intends that patriotism mean only admiration, let it be honest with itself and state its goals as follows: Patriotism (an uncritical love of the U.S., combined with harsh condemnation of those phenomena in American life supposedly at variance with pristine Americanism) and ability to think (except about the U.S.).

"If there are further areas in which thinking is to be limited, as there are in most communities, these too should be specified. Perhaps the most common would be:

—No type of thinking on religion would be fostered, even unintentionally, except that which agrees with the views of the parents concerned;

—The political values which pupils acquire must in no instance diverge from the political values of their parents;

—Sex will not be discussed, except to foster devotion to the mores (or, more precisely, the professed mores) of the adult community and except in ways sure to arouse no controversy.

"Our call for clarity is not far-fetched. Some communities have been so forthright as to prohibit, in writing, any teaching about evolution. Others outlaw teaching which might dispose pupils toward

24

conservation measures that conflict with commercial interests.

"To prohibit efforts to bias pupils toward the teacher's own views on these subjects is proper, for the teacher who profits from his position to bias his pupils mocks the goal of free and critical thinking. But the restrictions noted above, which are typical if unexpressed in communities throughout the country, are prohibitions of thought or of certain outcomes of thought.

"It is characteristic of adults to demand the perpetuation of their preferences and prejudices. Is this because they are certain that their preferences and prejudices are right? There are several possible answers. To answer yes would be unkind. To answer no would be equally unkind. A kinder answer would be that they merely fear that children, being immature, would be unable to arrive at the truth by their own thinking.

"Does it follow, however, that teachers and parents must bias children toward 'truths' that young minds cannot grasp? What is to be gained by indoctrination? Certainly, the ability to think is not fostered by the swallowing of absolute, incomprehensible conclusions. Having children learn 'the truth' now may even be incompatible with the hope that they will think for themselves later.

"Furthermore, if children are inculcated with an emotional, unreasoned patriotism or anti-evolutionism or any other philosophy, they may in the future be unable to handle conflicting evidence rationally. They may close their eyes to the evidence,

25

or react with anger, or conclude that the opposite extreme is right. That is, they may suffer a loss of realism or a loss of equanimity. And the entire nation will be the poorer, for the unthinking person is probably incapable, like many adults today, of combating or even recognizing the social flaws that threaten the way of life he supposedly cherishes.

"We are therefore convinced that many citizens who insist on the propagation of their preferences are deluding themselves. To impede a totally open search for reality is to hinder any worthy cause one may cherish.

"If we derive our goals of education from the spirit of science, our graduates will be patriotic in the highest sense. They will be dedicated to reflecting upon the social relevance of their values and actions, and to understanding and solving the problems that confront their fellow men."

There had never been much sentiment on the board for including patriotism among the goals of education. The statement was useful for another reason. It helped to convince the board that there was widespread support in the community for the view that unbridled thought was not un-American.

A SCHOOL IS BORN

"If academic incentives in this narrow sense tend to over-shadow intellectual incentives for most students, this is largely because the system of teaching so frequently is tuned to the desires of the academic strivers rather than to those of the intellectuals in the class. This is so for many reasons. One is that academically oriented instructions are easier to communicate to students, who usually want to know specifically what is expected of them in each course; it is hard to be specific about how to meditate and become wiser. . . . It is easier to throw the narrowly academic course requirements at one's students than it is to try to develop the frame of mind for embarking on a joint intellectual adventure. Also, the teacher has to give grades, and it is far simpler to assess narrowly academic achievement than to evaluate intel-lectual effort or reflective achievement."—Christian Bay, "Toward a Social Theory of Intellectual Development," in Nevitt Sanford (ed.), College and Character, *New York: John Wiley and Sons, 1964, p. 261.*

The school board's decision was to introduce a Chubb-type school one year at a time. Six-year-olds would be admitted in September, with a new group of six-year-olds each succeeding September. Thus, a declining number of children from Potseloo would attend school in Letlit each year, and children accustomed to the more rigid framework of education in Letlit would remain there.

As its first educational objectives, the board specified the seven elements of the spirit of science: *

—longing to know and to understand;

—questioning of all things;

—search for data and their meaning;

—demand for verification (though some deemed it unnecessary to mention both this goal and questioning of all things);

—respect for logic;

—consideration of premises;

—consideration of consequences.

The Board made three additions to the list. One was . . .

—creativity.

To some, this addition was superfluous, for they considered creativity part and parcel of several ingredients of the spirit of science. Thus, one teacher educator cited E. Paul Torrance, professor of educational psychology at the University of Georgia, who defined creativity in the school situation as ''a process whereby one becomes aware of problems, difficulties, gaps in information, and disharmonies for which he has no learned solution; searches for clues in the situation and existing knowledge, formulates hypotheses,

---

* See National Education Association and American Association of School Administrators, Educational Policies Commission, *Education and the Spirit of Science*. Washington, D. C.: The Commission, 1966. p. 15.

tests them, modifies and retests them; and communicates the results." However, in deference to those who feared that creativity risked being neglected if omitted from the list, no one actually opposed its insertion.

The next proposed addition was more controversial. State law and state board regulations ruled out the possibility of excluding all disciplines from lists of school objectives. Laws or regulations required the teaching of reading, writing, arithmetic, U. S. history, English literature and composition, physical education, the virtues of thrift, and the evils of narcotics, alcohol, and tobacco. Fortunately, neither the legislature nor the state board of education specified the grade levels at which these subjects must be taught or the amount of learning required, although for some subjects a minimum period of time was prescribed.

It was the opinion of the board that the laws and regulations would be satisfied by "reasonable" attention in each pupil's program to each of these areas. Where a minimum time period was prescribed, "reasonable" attention to the subject over that time period would suffice.

The ninth objective was worded:

—the broadest possible knowledge of the world, including due attention to those subjects required by state law and regulation.

While recognizing the legal requirements, Mr. Chubb saw danger in the chosen wording. "The broadest possible knowledge," he feared, could open the Pandora's box. It was fully consistent with the spirit of science: wasn't the broadest possible knowledge of the world inherent in the longing to know and the search for data? But this goal, thus worded, would be an open invitation to insistence on various and sundry pet subjects. Citizens who sensed neglect of their favorite subject (or of the latest fad) would start listing subjects and even itemizing content. "If the school submits to that pressure," Mr. Chubb warned, "the whole experiment is dead."

The board, however, reiterated its intention to keep educational objectives general. This intention, it insisted, did not imply a desire to transfer school control from the people to the teachers. On the contrary, it declared—persuasively indicating the extent of Mr. Chubb's triumph—that the schools could not carry out the public will unless the teachers were free to do their creative best. An educational objective could best be pursued by those in a position to take advantage of every opportunity to pursue it. Specificity as to methods, content, or deadlines by the public or by administrators would limit the teachers' ability to seize those opportunities. In deference to their own basic goals, citizens and administrators must carefully circumscribe their dictation to the schools.

Finally, the board added a tenth objective without opposition:

—development of sound bodies.

Not only was this objective considered intrinsically vital, but, as noted above, it was required by state law.

The board was agreed that the man most likely to be successful in breathing life into the new school was Mr. Chubb himself. It offered him the positions of principal and acting superintendent. Some Potselovians relished the chance to watch Mr. Chubb flounder in his efforts to translate his "utopian" ideas into reality. Some doubted his ability to practice what he preached in "keeping his nose out of the teachers' business." But most citizens wished him well. They shared—or longed to share—his faith in teachers and young people.

A SHOCKING PROPOSAL

Though eager to accept the twin offer, Mr. Chubb saw fit to jolt the board with a most unlikely proposal, a proposal so unorthodox and so selfless that some readers might come to doubt the very existence of Mr. Chubb.

The matter is so significant that failure to report it would be inexcusable.

Mr. Chubb proposed that the principal and acting superintendent be placed on the same salary schedule as the teachers. In his school, he explained, no one would make more decisions, more important decisions, or more demanding decisions, than the teachers themselves. In addition, a salary differential would promote the traditional hierarchical attitude, in which teachers feel subordinate to principals—a feeling both unjustified and detrimental.

"In factories," Mr. Chubb observed, "management consists of those who take the greatest risk, show the greatest initiative, and make the important decisions. Labor is there basically to carry out orders in return for a wage. But in a school, who is management and who is labor? In Potseloo, I hope, the distinction will be meaningless. I'll have to make certain decisions, such as whether our limited funds should be spent for new maps or more bus fares. The teachers will have to make others, most of them involving the question, 'What is the wisest way for Johnny to spend the next hour?' You'll readily agree that the decisions facing the teacher will be at least as complex as those facing me, and if anything they are more important.

"Why, then, should I be on a higher salary schedule than a teacher? This distinction might be proper in a school where the principal is the boss— the center of initiative and decision-making, and where the teacher is labor, doing a nine-to-four job. It seems to me that a school where it is right for a principal to get more than a teacher, for anything other than years of experience, is the wrong type of school."

Mr. Chubb lamented the fact that considerations of prestige and salary caused many teachers throughout the country to view success in their career as requiring a move from teaching to administration. If teaching came to be the delicate, expert, autonomous function here described, and came to be known as such, the prestige of teaching in the eyes of teachers and the public would perhaps rise appropriately. Salary differences between teaching and administration would have little reason to persist. And the best teachers would be able to remain in teaching.

Mr. Chubb's plea did not endear him with the principals in Letlit. Nor did it fully succeed. The board, though shocked, was impressed with the logic of its maverick administrator's request. However, after the grueling year of controversy which this same man's educational proposals had previously caused, the board shied away from further debate and from provoking further unrest in the once placid school system of neighboring Letlit. It therefore reaffirmed its original decision to pay teachers and principals the same as in Letlit, and to add a sizable bonus for the man acting as superintendent as well. Mr. Chubb agreed that the second job deserved a second salary; but he continued to maintain that the concept of a separate salary schedule was unhealthy.

MR. CHUBB'S LUCK PERSISTS

The Potseloo School opened with four first grades of 25 pupils each. Fortune smiled on it from the start. Teachers not only in Letlit but throughout the state and even beyond had heard of the experiment planned for Potseloo. Some Potselovians were enthusiastic supporters of the Chubb plan primarily because it had put Potseloo on the map. Two major companies even began investigating the advisability of establishing branches there.

Before any official announcement of the four openings for teachers, 15 primary teachers from Letlit and an equal number from other parts of the state had offered their services in writing or in person to Mr. Chubb. But numbers do not tell the best of the story. The 30 applicants were teachers who sought something other than the comfort of a well-planned routine. They were 26 women and four men who yearned to challenge their professional abilities to the fullest, who were not afraid to work at 25 different curriculums each day. The three women and one man whom Mr. Chubb selected were visibly outstanding in motivation, ability, and demeanor. They quickly won the people's confidence, assuring public respect for the experiment in its crucial first stages.

A second powerful factor operated in Mr. Chubb's favor. Curricular flexibility was characteristic of the primary level in the Letlit schools as well. It was not so total as in Potseloo, for Letlit pupils were expected by the end of each grade to have achieved at least the state average in each of several skills. But the shock of novelty in Potseloo was significantly diluted by the initial limitation of the experiment to six-year-olds.

The Hawthorne effect may also have contributed to the school's strong start and to its continuing success as a grade was added each year. The Hawthorne effect purportedly assures the success of virtually any experiment conducted with human participants as long as the participants are aware of being subjects of an experiment. In Potseloo, teachers and pupils could not but be aware of the spotlight focused on them from within the community and without.

As classes were added with each passing year, a further reason for high morale appeared. Chats with friends who attended school elsewhere quickly convinced Potseloo's pupils how lucky they were to be doing what they genuinely wanted to do in school.

36

PUBERTY RITES

There is an elementary education and there is a secondary education. This distinction is a basic fact of American life. What would Potseloo do to recognize the hallowed distinction as it approached its seventh or eighth year of life?

The decision virtually made itself when the time came. There had never been a self-contained, one-teacher classroom in the school. Teachers often brought in experts, sent children to the library or the laboratories, or assigned them temporarily to a teacher with special competence in a given subject or skill. Parents or teacher aides, or the teachers themselves, frequently accompanied children on field trips. Was a change in organization called for merely because the children had completed the sixth year of school and some of them had reached puberty?

In addition, it was noted, if the new facilities constructed for the older pupils were close-by, more laboratories and specialist teachers would be available to the younger pupils as well. Even in the primary grades, the pupils' free-ranging interests constantly created new needs for specialists and facilities.

In the eyes of many teachers, the possibility of expanding the teaching-pupil system was an equally cogent argument for maintaining a single school. The opportunity for pupils to teach and to participate in decisions on serious disciplinary problems was an essential aspect of education at Potseloo. Sometimes pupils had difficulties or interests in which they could be helped by older pupils or by their own classmates, and occasionally by younger pupils. Everyone benefitted by this system. Pupils can often relate to each other better than teachers can relate to them, whether in the learning process or in cases of breach of discipline (which in Potseloo usually meant violations of the rights or legitimate expectations of others, as interpreted by the pupils themselves). Pupils almost always wanted to prepare well for their teaching tasks; some of their best learning and thinking resulted from the need to explain to others. In addition, they were proud of the confidence shown in them. Yet manifestations of arrogance were rare in these relationships, since each tutor sometimes found himself in the role of tutee as well, and since the teachers' tact and counseling skill helped to assure healthy relationships.

Obviously, the addition of higher grades to the same school offered an excellent opportunity to expand the teaching-pupil system.

Since curricular decisions were normally made through consultation between pupil and teacher, it was natural for teachers to consult pupils before making a recommendation on new construction as well.

The fifth and sixth graders' opinions correlated strikingly with the length of their experience at the Potseloo school. Those who were new to the school for the most part favored a separate high school. They evidently preferred not to prolong their association with "the babies." On the other hand, those who had been in Potseloo from the beginning—and these were the majority—were generally either indifferent or in favor of expansion of the existing school. The Potseloo youngsters were less in need than others of special homage to their superior age. Respect for their dignity as individuals and recognition of their individual level of development had, from the beginning, permeated the making of all decisions affecting them. They needed no separate building as a fortress for their self-esteem.

The school board decided to build the new facilities adjacent to the old, with enclosed hallways joining the two buildings on each of the two floors. Elementary and secondary grades would be located in both buildings.

Thus, there continued to be a single Potseloo school, a twelve-year institution. When asked, some seventh-year pupils would reply that they were in high school; others would say simply that they were in the seventh year. When a year has passed, all pupils can legitimately make only one *common* statement—that they have been in school for one year more. Other claims, such as "I am a seventh grader" or "I am in high school," are technically correct; but they are likely to imply a fiction, for they imply a common level of achievement.

DOES JOHNNY TEND MORE OFTEN
TO QUESTION WHAT HE HEARS AND READS? . . .
(See page 42).

CHAPTER II

The essence of the system

"In artistic creation, diversity of styles, methods, and genres is inevitable. We oppose efforts to level off the individual peculiarities of artists. The Party and people desire just one thing: that works of art reflect the living truth, reveal the greatness of the heroic feats of the Soviet people, educate everyone in the spirit of communism's lofty ideals and help them implement those ideals."—From speech by Leonid I. Brezhnev to All-Union Congress of Teachers, quoted in Sovetskaya Pedagogika (*Soviet Teaching*), *Aug. '68. p. 13.*

The essence of the Potseloo system is this: in consultation with each pupil, the teachers try at all times to construct a program consistent with his interests and with the ten basic goals of education as established by the school board.

No syllabus or textbook provides the basis for a teacher's relationship with his pupils. Neither does any future examination. Most students will eventually need to pass college entrance exams, but the teachers are convinced that their system, operating without external guides, will lead most pupils to a level of achievement far surpassing college entrance requirements.

Rather, each teacher's efforts are guided by these questions:

1. Does Johnny show a growing curiosity about the world?
2. Does Johnny tend more often and more maturely to question his own thoughts and beliefs and what he hears and reads?
3. Does Johnny seek to satisfy his curiosity with growing persistence and maturity?
4. Does Johnny insist on verification before accepting assertions?
5. Does Johnny apply logic in his thinking?
6. Does Johnny try to be aware of his premises and to evaluate them?
7. Does Johnny consider the likely consequences of his actions and beliefs?
8. Is Johnny becoming more creative in his thinking and his actions?
9. Is Johnny's knowledge of the world becoming deeper and broader?
10. Is Johnny developing the strength, health, and fitness of his body and increasing his ability to do so on his own?

Group activities are invaluable for many of these purposes, such as developing awareness of one's premises, developing new areas of curiosity, or learning to defend and sharpen one's logic. But individuals are not assigned to learning groups for the teacher's convenience.

At Potseloo, concern for ten goals of fundamental importance to each pupil's life is not adulterated by the need to communicate previously delineated subject matter. Advance decisions are not made to teach any given subject, fact, idea, or skill to any pupil at any given time. Yet the teachers deal constantly with the content of subjects, for logic is exercised on content, curiosity is about content, views consist of content, and problems and their solutions are about content. Therefore, the pupils quickly immerse themselves in knowledge, and hence in the skills they need to acquire and comprehend that knowledge. But they immerse themselves in the boundless ocean of knowledge and skills, not in a pool roped off ahead of time.

Most Potesloo pupils become vigorous swimmers in their ocean, while in pools elsewhere, where the lanes are clearly marked, many of their fellows lose interest in swimming. Human beings seem to thrive in the ocean of knowledge which they have created. They do not fare nearly so well in captivity.

CAN WE RELY
ON PUPILS' INTERESTS?

"Student government has grown apace, students now not only governing themselves but giving valuable suggestions, in the form of ultimatums, to the President and Dean."—Richard Armour, Going around in Academic Circles, *New York: McGraw-Hill Book Company, 1965. Used with permission of McGraw-Hill Book Company.*

In its first two or three years the Potseloo experiment, relying on pupils' interests, was incontrovertibly a success. Doubters could explain this initial success with the observation, "Little children will be genuinely interested in almost anything you suggest."

But total reliance on pupils' interests in later years generally seemed absurd, both to professional educators and to lay people. They feared that most students, of their own accord, would show little interest—or at least little steadfast interest—in anything useful. A related, if less desperate, pessimism led others to predict that some vital skills or areas

44

of knowledge would be neglected if individual interests, rather than pre-set plans, were always the point of departure.

Experience at Potseloo does support the latter pessimism. Some pupils do remain ignorant in areas on which they ought to be informed—but only because there is a virtual infinity of worthwhile areas. No system of education has ever avoided these gaps. No conceivable system could, at least in the present state of the art of education.

The more far-reaching pessimism is virtually inapplicable to Potseloo. It is provoked by that powerful, if often misleading, persuader—experience. Millions of teachers and parents have witnessed the tragic metamorphosis which occurs when initially alert, questioning children discover that school is a place to satisfy not curiosity, but teachers, parents, principals, and college entrance authorities. Childish curiosity gives way to the cramming syndrome. Serious learning, once a means of relating to what one perceived as the real world, becomes the execution of tasks imposed by people who know better. As John Dewey, the great American educator and philosopher, lamented, the world ceases to be the unified, vivid object of one's perceptions and becomes a clump of discrete, cold compartments called subjects.

No wonder our schools have taught us the untruth that most human beings will learn only with a stick behind them or a carrot in front!

The experience of our schools hinders the ability of adults to sense the infinite promise inherent in young people's own, genuine interests. The fact is that, with proper guidance, virtually any interest can lead to learning in many different areas, regardless of a pupil's age. For example, the subject of space flight is technological and scientific. But it is also a matter of international rivalry, a manifestation of a society's economic development, a result of political decisions, and a case study in the goals of life. An interest in space flight can lead to learning in any of these fields; or in mathematics, or in the writing of science fiction, or in speculation about the future.

Some Potseloo pupils, of course, derive no abiding interest or significant learning from their initial enthusiasm about space flight. But they are motivated by some other subject—sports, food, poverty, China, conservation, presidential elections, television, religion, or virtually any other phenomenon in the world. Each of these interests can be a way station to learning to read, studying history or literature, or dozens of other skills and areas of knowledge.

Often a child does not announce his interest clearly. But more interests are "there" than can ever be exploited. They are waiting for a teacher to bring them out. And those interests are reliable bases for learning, since they are in the pupils' minds, not in the teacher's plans.

It is a disheartening fact that many educators and other citizens, upon first hearing about the Potseloo school, immediately conceive of it as obsessed with fun, with making everything easy for fear that the children will otherwise lose interest. Like John Dewey, Potseloo is often unjustly thought to favor whimsical activity over hard work. "Oh, yes," we are told, "youngsters have plenty of interests. But if those interests start involving work, they quickly evaporate."

Young people, it is true, often want to play, relax, and avoid serious thinking. So, by the way, do adults. It is also true that, when confronted with a task that they find unappealing, youngsters are genuinely motivated to find an easy way to do it.

In the proper circumstances, however, their capacity for intense work is as great as their capacity for intense play. As psychologists Abraham H. Maslow and Jean Piaget have pointed out, youngsters like to grow and exercise their capacities. They are willing to work hard—even to struggle—at any task which has integral importance for them. Watch a child struggle with the waves to build a sand castle. Watch your daughter prepare for an important date, or your son try out for the football team. Watch a student cram for a final exam, or a young person learn to smoke or drink, distasteful as he finds it at first. Watch a teenager work at a hobby.

Teachers at Potseloo have found that the longing to know and the longing to grow are motivations as powerful in young people as having fun, winning prestige, or passing a course.

Potseloo has its most consistent trouble with transfer students. Recognizing that the curriculum will largely depend upon them, they sometimes plan

47

to "take advantage" of the new situation by loafing. School and family have taught them that the real purpose for bothering to learn is to avoid a failing grade, please the teacher, win praise or avoid punishment from their parents, maintain their personal prestige, gain admission to college, or get the assignment over with. Basically, they have learned in response to what B. F. Skinner, professor of psychology at Harvard University, calls "aversive control"— the desire to avoid punishment—which, as he argues, is both inefficient and incompatible with human dignity. They have learned a few facts or concepts, at least for a time. But they have not learned to dedicate themselves for a lifetime to the pursuit of objectivity or to any other goal that will assist them or matter to them throughout their lives. They have learned to learn on command. They want directions.

The recovery of the transfer students begins with their amazement upon discovering that a teacher considers their own interests honorable. Their incredulity betrays a tragically revealing question: "If I actually want to learn everything I am learning, can I be learning the right things?"

Severe misbehavior is rarely a problem. Why rebel against a system that obviously respects you? For many of the older pupils, the Potseloo school is a haven from the indignities that society visits upon adolescents. Society tends to treat young people, throughout their long adolescence, as political, economic, and sexual children. At Potseloo, on the other hand, they are given considerable responsibility early in life for all their activities. That school, unlike most, appears to the teenager as the one social institution that really listens to him. This respect may account for the fact that few of them bother to learn to smoke. They evidently feel less need than most adolescents to demonstrate their "adulthood."

THE IMPACT OF A GIVEN EVENT ON ANY TWO PUPILS IS AS INDIVIDUAL AS THEIR FINGERPRINTS . . .
(See page 53).

FEAR OF
CHAOS AND IMBALANCE

According to newspaper reports, a principal in Washington, D. C., has accused a young teacher of committing virtually unspeakable sins in her efforts to reach her pupils. She failed, he alleged, to follow the curriculum on which her administrators insisted, and—incredible as it sounds—she even resorted to teaching materials which were not on the approved list of the curriculum department. Though this rigidly upstanding administrator and his unforgivably creative hired hand received publicity in the press, countless unsung principals have rebuked countless unsung teachers for the same inane reasons.

In these disputes, however, teachers find many of their colleagues in the opposing camp. Thousands of teachers would undoubtedly agree that a school system would plunge into chaos if each teacher went off in a different direction, doing as he pleased. And is it not obvious that the chaos would be still worse if each pupil's activities were decided upon from moment to moment? How much neater (and, incidentally, more convenient) is a curriculum that is planned and that consists of subjects, even if subjects are no longer defined as conglomerations of correct answers, which was the ultimate in neatness (and convenience)! Imagine how unbalanced a curriculum would be, overemphasizing some areas and neglecting others, if balance is not specifically planned!

No wars are waged at Potseloo over the problem of balance—over the relative place of this or that subject in the curriculum. The humanities and the sciences are not loggerheads. How can a subject jockey for position when the position of each subject for each pupil can be determined only as his interests develop? How can the physics teacher fight with the literature teacher or with the artist for a larger slice of the pupil's school day or school year when there are no assigned courses and no decisions in advance as to how much of what field anyone will study?

Moreover, it is the task of each teacher, in view of the ninth goal of education at Potseloo, to foster a wide range of learning from each pupil's interests. If one teacher does not direct him to a given subject, another teacher may. Of course, no two pupils will learn an equal amount of any given subject, but no system achieves that result. And why bother to try? There are more worthy goals to pursue.

However, the problem of balance is not totally self-solving at Potseloo. By virtue of their own specialized knowledge and interests, some teachers tend to direct pupils more toward activities in the humanities than in the sciences, more toward mathematics than toward art, more toward ethical speculation than international relations. One of the principal's main jobs is to develop programs that will broaden each teacher's awareness of the world. His purpose is not directly to alter the teachers' patterns of choice, but rather to expand their range of vision, and hence their range of choice.

In practice, the restraints which a teacher's knowledge imposes upon his range of choice are not grave if he knows the resources of his school and his community. When children express interests patently outside the teacher's personal knowledge, he need only know where to go for help or where to send the children for help. Moreover, in helping children to follow up on such interests, and later on in discussing their progress with the children and their new helpers, a teacher necessarily expands his own awareness of the world. Teaching at Potseloo is a permanent learning experience. Giving the same course year after year has been eliminated as a blight on professional life there.

So much for the problem of imbalance. But what of chaos?

A description of a single day's program in the Potseloo school would certainly take many more pages than a similar description for most other schools. The obvious reason is that at Potseloo a separate tale would have to be told about each pupil. But let us redefine "program" to mean, not the visible activities of pupils, but the changes that take place in their minds. In that case, a separate tale would have to be told each day about any two pupils in any school, for the impact of a given event on any two pupils is as individual as their fingerprints. In the true sense, then, Potseloo is not more chaotic than any other school; it just looks that way. It looks that way because we often interpret education to mean a visible program rather than an impact.

Therefore, when one describes education at Potseloo as more chaotic than education elsewhere, one is talking only about appearances. Unquestionably, the visible activities there are extraordinarily diverse.

Potseloo cannot satisfy those who see education as necessarily implying a large degree of uniform experiences for all pupils. Yet, if planning is the antithesis of chaos, Potseloo is orderly.

At Potseloo, no decision is made in advance that groups of children will learn the same things at the same time or, indeed, will cover any given material in the course of their school career. But this does not mean that learning activities take place without planning or preparation. On the contrary, the necessary amount of planning and preparation is colossal.

The basic problem, after all, is to be prepared to satisfy any of a potentially infinite number of interests and convert each of them into a long-range gain for health, creativity, or the spirit of science. The main difficulty in such a system is an insatiable demand for learning aids and experts. They are needed not only for every topic, but for every level of maturity and every type of background. Potseloo's experience accords with what some psychologists have long suspected—that any subject or concept can be taught in an intellectually honest way even to little children. Therefore, every interest is educationally valid at every age.

Potseloo hungers for every new material that industry and scholarship can conceivably provide on every topic. It eagerly awaits the day when a computer system will give instantaneous access to much of the world's knowledge and to nearly complete information on the availability of learning materials.

Much of the needed expertise is supplied by citizens of the community. Most citizens and agencies are willing, indeed eager and honored, to contribute their special skills to the education of the young. They approach each new relationship with confidence because they know that the pupils come to them with sincerity, in fulfillment of a need recognized by the pupils rather than in obedience to a requirement imposed by adults. A citizen with something to offer cannot be really happy with an audience of captives, or with an audience glad to be there only because it regards the field trip as a welcome relief from less pleasant requirements.

The use of outside agencies and individuals requires considerable preparation. First, mutually convenient times must be established. A school wedded to the traditional school day, with pupils afflicted by the usual attitudes toward school, could not often turn to the community for help. But the time set aside for "formal" education at Potseloo is flexible. The basic school day, school week, and school year are precisely those of the rest of the state. With the exception of the opening day in September, however, pupils are actually in the classroom or school only by agreement with their teachers: that is, only as their learning activities require. An assignment chosen by a pupil and a teacher which can most conveniently be executed on an evening, weekend, or holiday is regarded as normal. It is not considered as homework, for there is little reason to distinguish classwork from homework. Much school time is spent outside the school building, or in the building with outside specialists, and all of it is spent at activities which the pupil himself wants, or whose need he genuinely recognizes. Therefore, school and relaxation, or learning and enjoyment, are not so distinct from each other as in most school systems. In these circumstances, it is relatively easy to find times in which non-school personnel can assist pupils in their learning activities.

Preparation for this assistance involves more than finding a mutually convenient time. It also involves assistance by the teacher to the person who is going to help. In particular, the teacher needs to provide relevant background on the pupil concerned. He must, for example, provide information on the methods that seem most helpful with that pupil. He needs to describe the relationship of the planned activity to the pupil's overall program as it has developed to date. And he needs to reach agreement with the community helper and the pupil on the preparation which the pupil should undertake.

The Potseloo school would be incomparably poorer without these community contributions. It is not just that pupils would make less progress toward the goals of the school. People seem to derive great satisfaction from service—from the knowledge that they can contribute. The exceptional solidarity between citizen and school which visitors notice in Potseloo does not derive just from the fact that the school has put Potseloo on the map. It derives still more from the technical assistance which the community is called upon to give. To make a citizen an occasional teacher is to make an outsider an insider.

Some school systems approach the citizenry only when the time comes to raise taxes or approve bond issues. Potseloo asks the citizens for assistance all year. Some schools try to keep the citizenry informed of their programs. Potseloo makes the citizenry an integral, indispensable part of its program.

Pupils, for their part, derive from each experience in the community something more than progress toward the school's ten objectives. They acquire a deepened awareness that school and community are united—that learning and life are one.

Actually, this awareness may be an indispensable ingredient in love of learning.

WHAT WOULD IT MEAN TO SAY
THAT JOE HAS COMPLETED FIFTH-GRADE REQUIREMENTS
IN "AWARENESS OF PREMISES?" . . .
(See page 67).

PLANNING BY TEACHERS

Much planning is directed toward the acquisition of new materials and the facilitation of community assistance. But the lion's share of planning is that which takes place between teachers and pupils.

As previously indicated, some teachers at Potseloo who have specialized in a given field try just a little harder to develop pupils' interest in that field, to promote understanding of its basic concepts or, as urged by Jerome S. Bruner, Director of the Center for Cognitive Studies at Harvard University, to help pupils imbibe its spirit and methodology. But it is each teacher's job, whatever his biases, to keep the proper ten questions in mind at all times.

Perhaps the skill most needed by all the teachers is that of seeing and seizing opportunities for the progress of their pupils toward the ten goals. The teachers must then decide how to exploit the opportunity—how much supervision a pupil needs in the course of the activity, the extent to which group work is appropriate and feasible, and how to advance the various facets of the spirit of science when the pupil's only motive is interest in something specific and factual.

These decisions are normally complicated by the circumstance that the pupil is already in the midst of one useful activity when he displays a new interest. The teacher must help the pupil decide whether the pupil's time would best be spent by persisting in his present activity, by switching to a new one (perhaps with a different teacher), or by a combination of the two.

The result of all these decisions will be a planned, individualized activity which may terminate in 15 minutes or continue for years.

On its regular staff Potseloo employs teachers specialized in those fields which have proved to be most in demand. These are, for the most part, the subjects in which schools traditionally concentrate.

The primary teachers are specialized in teaching reading and writing and in using these activities to promote progress toward the ten objectives. They are practiced, for example, in helping children to ask questions. They are also skilled in teaching children the elementary use of numbers and a sense of mathematics.

Throughout all the years of his schooling, a pupil is likely to need history and biology teachers. Young people who are encouraged to wonder want to know why society is as it is and are restlessly curious about living things, including their own bodies, health, sex, and death.

Other regular areas of concern are the physical sciences, economics, linguistics, sociology, psychology, anthropology, politics, philosophy, and foreign languages. Art and industrial arts teachers are much in demand. The physical educators, though not enjoying a monopoly as purveyors of fun, are constantly busy. They seek, as in most schools, to develop sound bodies and to provide for the expenditure of youthful energy in healthful, enjoyable ways. Their purposes are also intellectual—to stimulate thinking about the relationship between health and fitness; to make pupils thoughtful about the ways they choose to spend their time, and to develop motivations which will keep even desk workers fit for the rest of their lives. They sometimes work closely with biology teachers to develop a knowledge of muscles, glands, or lungs, and their functioning. Frequently they engage pupils in discussions of ethics and loyalty.

The teacher of auto mechanics and driver training often works with the teachers of physics and chemistry to help pupils understand, for example, what makes motors go and why lubricants work. He takes advantage of the opportunities which driver training incessantly provides to develop pupils' interest in local government, federal regulation of private enterprise, and even comparative government. At every point, he encourages pupils to ask why, rather than merely to do as told.

The sculptor, painter, and music teacher provide some pupils with an important basis for healthy development of the rational powers, for these activities constitute an emotional outlet as powerful for some people as are sports, religion, or love. The teachers sometimes use the arts as a springboard for inquiry into oneself, into human values, into the past, into other cultures, and into the nature of truth. For example, pupils may ponder whether Dostoevski teaches us something about life, Russia, the past, or himself. The incandescence, the profound emotional participation and joy, which great art has elicited over the centuries becomes, in the hands of a master teacher, not only an end in itself, but also a stimulus to inquiry into the why of that joy and the role it should play in one's life. The teachers also use education in the arts to help pupils experience life in the full—that is, to make them sensitive to the beauty and ugliness in human relations and in nature.

Finally, the arts are used to develop creativity and imagination. But these domains are not reserved to art teachers. In schools pervaded by authoritarianism and tension, pupils prefer the snug haven of traditional, approved responses. But at Potseloo, the relative lack of emphasis on competitive success and failure leaves pupils at ease and fosters creativity in all their learning activity.

PUPIL GROUPING

Are classes better if they are homogenized, containing only the cream or only the lighter minds? Or is ability grouping useless or even harmful? These questions have agitated educators for decades. Yet the problem of student grouping virtually solved itself at Potseloo.

When a six-year old enrolls in the school, he is assigned to a homeroom. The first-year homeroom teachers are those who prefer to teach the basic skills and who enjoy working with little children. Whatever the children's interests, one of the means for satisfying some of them, at least by the second year, is arithmetic. Another is reading. Often the ability to read is itself an objective of the pupils. In many cases, the primers are brief materials prepared by the homeroom teachers in cooperation with teachers or community helpers who are experts in the various fields. An impressive collection of such materials, some of them in special alphabets, has been accumulated over the years, freeing teachers from dependence on traditional, often uninspiring, mass-produced readers. Most children learn to write as they learn to read.

Children normally remain with the same homeroom teacher for two, three, or four years. However, teachers may at any time agree to transfer pupils between them, or even to surrender their classes *in toto*. Individual transfers occur in response to hostility between pupils, a difficulty that a teacher and a pupil have in working with each other, or a desire for more variety in the composition of the class. Total transfers generally occur because the class has outgrown its basic need for the teacher's specialty—namely, teaching elementary reading. The teacher would prefer a younger class, in which he can utilize his special skill.

Most children have a wide variety of contacts during their first year at Potseloo. In subsequent years they spend more and more of their time with teachers other than their homeroom teacher and in places other than their homeroom, for other people can help them more in many of the subjects that interest them. By the time they are 11, 12, or 13 years of age, their presence in the homeroom is only spasmodic. But the homeroom teacher continues to be responsible for discussing with parents each pupil's progress and problems, or for coordinating that discussion between parents and teachers. As pupils enter their final years, the homeroom teacher has the additional task of sounding the alarm when a pupil's record indicates a failure to meet subject requirements of state law or college entrance. Each September, the homeroom teacher is also responsible for guiding the pupils to their initial activities.

The question of ability grouping does not even arise. In the homeroom it would be irrelevant, since pupils remain together for most of their learning activities only in the very first year or two. In other cases, pupil interests are the decisive factors in assigning them to teachers. Pupils often work in groups on a project, or teachers organize group discussions to develop awareness of premises, to discover gaps in knowledge or logic, and to acquaint pupils with each other's interests. Grouping may be designed to achieve either variety or uniformity of interests, but grouping by ability is relevant only occasionally, for the facilitation of specific group projects.

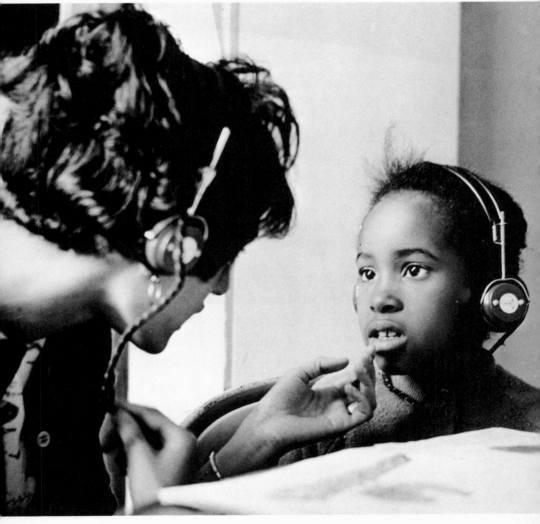

THE CHEMISTRY OF RELATIONSHIPS
BETWEEN A PUPIL AND A TEACHER IS
INFINITELY COMPLEX . . .
(See page 72).

PUPIL EVALUATION

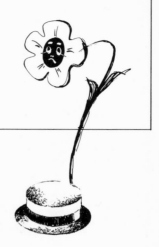

"How can we reduce the number of failures while at the same time eliminating the unwritten rule which guides some schools: a 'C' on his report card, a 'D' in his head?"— Sovetskaya Pedagogika (*Soviet Teaching*), *Apr. '68. p. 14.*

Each teacher's professional skill is challenged to the utmost in the process of evaluation.

Evaluation is an assessment of progress toward stated goals. In most schools, it is usually a measure of the accumulation of knowledge or the accumulation and the understanding of knowledge. Thus, a final mark of 80% in a geometry course presumably indicates that the pupil has memorized (and, in the better cases, understood) about four-fifths of the geometry that the class covered.

In the context of the goals at Potseloo, however, numerical and letter grades and the concept of grade level are absurd. What would it mean to assert that Sally has achieved a "B" in "questioning all things?" What would be the sense of the statement that Joe is ready for the sixth grade because he has completed fifth-grade requirements in "awareness of premises?" Could there be such a phenomenon as 100% in "longing to know and to understand?" Against what ideal standard will "creativity" be measured? As for "the broadest possible knowledge," every person's knowledge of the world is so individual that it would be an infinitely complex task to measure one pupil's knowledge against another's.

At Potseloo, then, evaluation cannot be a neat measurement. The teachers are not grief-stricken by this impossibility; educators have long recognized that the type of competitive motivation that arises from the traditional grading system is unhealthy. But what alternative is there?

Evaluation at Potseloo usually results from discussion between teacher and pupil. At one or more points during an activity planned specifically for and with a pupil, he meets with the specialist or homeroom teacher to discuss his progress and problems. In the course of the discussion, the teacher tries to discern answers to such questions as these:

—Is Fred insisting on evidence more frequently?
—Is his use of logic improving so that he can more keenly discern whether his evidence is relevant and adequate to his conclusions?
—Is he questioning the assertions of books and people, as well as his own beliefs, more maturely than before?

—Has he learned new ways to search for data?

—Has he found the experience rewarding enough that he will want to pursue learning in this field or in a related field?

Naturally, a teacher cannot answer these questions with numerical precision. He can summarize, in the pupil's records and in letters or discussions with parents, the extent of the pupil's progress toward the goals of the school. The hope is that each pupil will have promoted himself a little each day. There is no concept of annual promotion. There are merely twelve years of pursuit of progress.

An evaluation session may involve a third person—another teacher, a community helper, a parent, or a teaching pupil. A group of pupils may also participate if their presence is thought to be beneficial.

A most beneficial form of evaluation occurs when the teacher knows little about the discipline involved, for in such cases the pupil teaches the teacher some content.

Evaluation sessions at Potseloo tell teachers much about their own ability. They are effective programs of in-service training. Teachers are able to assess what they have done well and what they might have done better. They agree that the evaluation sessions are more productive than some of the in-service courses they take at the college in Letlit.

Evaluation sessions are the groundwork for planning the pupil's next activity. Should he proceed along the same path, perhaps with some modifications? Or is a totally new activity called for?

The primary criterion of a good evaluation session is the extent to which it is a learning experience for the pupil. It should produce further understanding of the subject, of methods, and of self. It should generally intensify interest. At the teacher's discretion a test may be given, but the threat of evaluation must never become part of a pupil's motivation. Occasionally, teachers at Potseloo have earned the reputation of relying on tests to motivate pupils. In each such case, two consequences have quickly occurred. First: the teacher's clientele diminishes, or the number of pupils remaining with him for extended assignments declines. Second: the principal and other teachers rush to the rescue of their afflicted colleague with suggestions. This is one example of Potseloo's system of merit rating.

A MERIT SYSTEM THAT PROBABLY
REWARDS MERIT

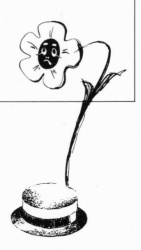

The merit system at Potseloo developed spontaneously. It appears to be inherent in the concept of education that reigns there. The school adheres to the normal pattern of salary increments for experience and further study. Its merit system has nothing to do with salaries. In fact, it rewards merit with additional work. Yet it is most compelling.

Every teacher is assigned a homeroom. Here, and here alone, he has a captive audience. Together with each pupil, the homeroom teacher makes the initial decisions in September which send the pupils off to various learning activities including, perhaps, some under the homeroom teacher's own guidance. When the next teacher, teaching pupil, or community teacher concludes that his work with the pupil is completed, or that the pupil should embark simultaneously on another activity, he discusses the matter with the homeroom teacher. Evaluation sessions, too, may involve more than one teacher, as noted previously.

Through these discussion sessions, the teachers become acquainted with each other's methods, attitudes, and results. Mr. Chubb regards these sessions as superb in-service training opportunities. He urges the teachers to make suggestions to each other freely and to consider each other's suggestions seriously. But if a teacher concludes that a colleague works poorly with pupils in general or with one pupil in particular, he will use his influence to see to it that future activities of those pupils, or that pupil, avoid the given colleague.

Naturally, the pupil himself, after one unfortunate experience, may try to avoid further contact with that teacher. One of the most vital, sensitive, and common counseling functions which teachers at Potseloo must perform is that of assuring that avoidance of a teacher stems from factors truly relevant to the school's goals. Sometimes, the ostensible basis for a pupil's complaint is that a given teacher overworks him. On further investigation, however, this explanation generally proves superficial. Overwork is in part a state of mind. Potseloo pupils work hard in most of their assignments. If they are conscious of overwork, it is probably because they dislike what they are doing. Herein lies the key to recognizing poor teaching, at least at Potseloo. Poor teaching is above all the ability to convert a pupil's genuine interest into dislike and boredom. Of course, this criterion is applicable only where genuine interest is the starting point; it would rarely work in most schools.

Mr. Chubb tries to keep alive a spirit which elicits from all teachers the most sincere efforts to help a pupil and teacher who are having trouble with each other. But eventually, poor teaching is reflected in a decline in business. The drop is particularly devastating when there is more than one teacher of the same specialty. The clientele of one grows, and that of the other declines.

Some teachers who do little for most pupils do wonders for a few. The chemistry of relationships between a pupil and a teacher is infinitely complex. Indeed, Mr. Chubb suspects on occasion that the very elements in a teacher's character which reduce his compatibility with some pupils generate the sparks which ignite the intellect of others. It is the principal's task to see to it that the competencies and achievements of each teacher, as of each pupil, are recognized and respected. Teachers are just as much individuals as are pupils.

This judgment by the market-place has several advantages over the usual forms of evaluation of teachers. First, it is based on professional performance. Second, it is a judgment made not because regulations or job descriptions require someone to make it, but because it is a natural part of one's work. Third, making the judgment does not occupy the time of someone who ought to be doing something else. Fourth, it is the judgment of many of one's colleagues, not just of one. Most teachers are evaluated differently by different colleagues and pupils; what is significant is a judgment widely shared by one's colleagues and pupils, it being understood that a low rating may be offset by great effectiveness with a few pupils.

Naturally, other reasons may account for a change in the number of students congregating to a teacher. In particular, world, national, or local trends or fads may boost or break the popularity of a subject. The principal therefore apprises himself closely of circumstances before rushing to aid or praise a teacher. But teachers know why they hesitate to send pupils to a colleague, or why they are eager to do so. A major job of the principal is to strengthen the atmosphere of mutual confidence and helpfulness among teachers. He calls faculty meetings only when there is genuine cause; he does not need such meetings to keep staff members in contact with one another when the breadth of children's interests virtually guarantees that every teacher will have significant professional contact with most other teachers in the course of the year. His efforts are directed at making these contacts genuinely helpful. He informs all candidates for teaching positions that mutual criticism plays a major role at Potseloo. Teaching, he says, is too significant to let personal sensitivities stand in the way of improvement. Recent college graduates, fresh from the ordeal of student teaching, are not perturbed. Old timers, however, must sometimes learn that, in the proper climate, suggestions can be given in kindness. Creation of this climate depends above all on the principal.

CHAPTER III

From sex to status

To think of an education system which encourages all questions and all interests, and to think
at the same time of teenagers, is to think of a sex-
dominated curriculum. This, I suspect, is one of the
main, if usually unexpressed, sources of hostility to a
truly free education.

It is true that many pupils develop curiosity in
areas which make adults squeamish. In ascending
order of delicacy, these areas are ideology, politics,
religion, and sex.

The experience of the Potseloo school indicates
that the keys to educational success and community
acceptance in these areas are the pursuit of objectivity
and the effort to keep the public informed of activities.

Parents soon see that pupils who understand
rather than memorize the meaning of freedom, and
who see it function around them, do not tend to

choose the ideologies or policies of tyranny. At first, many parents are apprehensive about an atmosphere in which rebellion is not outlawed and conformity is not demanded; but they are regularly invited to classes in which they see thought at work. They see the evolving thought of their children submitted to the consideration of other pupils. They feel reassured upon observing that rebellion as well as conformity is made to submit to thought. True thought seems to have a leavening effect. Some of its implications are revolutionary, but in a calm way. The recognition of injustice, for example, leads the thoughtful man to search for ways to harmonize the need for change with the need for order. Questioning of religion leads to reflection on man's desire for a closer connection with the universe and an understanding of life.

In short, the question raised by George S. Counts in 1932—whether the schools dare build a new social order—does not really present itself at Potseloo, for Potseloo does not furnish answers. It merely fosters the ability to reach one's own thoughtful conclusions on fundamental problems of man and society.

Sex, however, is the most pregnant of all subjects in embarrassing implications.

SEX

If every deceived husband and wife carried a lamp, what illumination there would be!

—Italian Proverb

"The school and family must prepare not only the future citizen, but the future family member as well—the husband and father, the wife and mother. In this regard we must, of course, renounce the negative attitude toward sex education. Let us be frank: the extreme inattentiveness to questions of sexual development of children and youth, the substitution of 'self-education' for the wise, tactful sex education of young people causes moral damage to our young people."— Sovetskaya Pedagogika (*Soviet Teaching*), *April 1968. p. 122.*

Questions of sex arise at all ages. They become most insistent, of course, at adolescence. Most of the teachers at Potseloo have concluded that attention to sex can be repressed in school only at the cost of invaluable learning opportunities. They have further concluded that the subject is indeed being repressed unless considerable school time is devoted to it by adolescents.

Most schools seem to regard sex as a distraction from true education. Must educators seize every opportunity to convince youngsters that what really matters to them is immaterial or even dangerous to the school?

Perhaps most schools could not grant to adolescents as much freedom to study the subject of sex as Potseloo does. By the age of 12 to 14, children there have developed considerable sophistication in asking questions and seeking answers. They have already developed, within themselves, standards that keep their inquiry worthwhile. Despite their burning interest, they are able to apply the same standards to the study of sex. Some squeamishness is evident in group discussions and teacher-pupil discussions of the subject; but most pupils develop a considerable understanding of the "mysteries" of sex, and learn to hold this facet of life in high esteem.

In school as in life, a concern for sex stimulates extensive and often intensive interest in other matters, such as poetry, human development, sociology, the population explosion, the physiology of humans and other animals, anthropology, and ethics. There is no stronger basis for progress toward self-awareness, consideration of consequences, and understanding of the world.

Potseloo, of course, possesses no regular, planned program in sex education. The school is too intent upon education to heed the advice of the U.S.

Office of Education or the American Association of
School Administrators that a special program on the
subject be established. Yet Potseloo is probably one
of the few schools in the United States which gives
sex education its due.

GIVING EVERY TEACHER THE OPPORTUNITY TO
ACT LIKE A PROFESSIONAL . . .
(See page 87).

COLLEGE ADMISSION REQUIREMENTS

Like all schools, Potseloo has needed from the start to contend with cases of inadequate persistence in learning and lack of enthusiasm for subjects required by law or by college entrance authorities. Sometimes, for example, students who need a foreign language for admission to college have little interest in learning a language or in persisting at it long enough to meet minimum requirements. What alternative is there, then, to enforcement of a three- or four-year language requirement at Potseloo?

Mr. Chubb would react with a tirade against the colleges or the legislature responsible for the requirement. Admittedly, a student who knows a foreign language can do more than a student who does not. However, the same could be said for any subject. No one—not even so august a being as a college entrance authority—can be sure that a foreign language will do more for a given student, or for the college, than would a knowledge of paper-making or anthropology. These doubts would be justified even if students tended less consistently to refrain from any worthy use whatsoever of the linguistic skills they acquire in school or college.

Potseloo satisfies with ease most of the requirements established by law and by college authorities. They relate to subjects in which pupils normally display interest anyway, and they do not specify the knowledge required. But the foreign-language requirement has been troublesome. Unmotivated students can achieve the required level of competence only through tedious rote memorization. Virtually all students at Potseloo develop an interest in other tongues, but not all continue for long to study them with gusto.

A person forced to pursue studies which he no longer wishes to pursue is likely to study inefficiently. "Why require inefficiency?" ask Mr. Chubb and others. In particular, why require inefficiency when the time spent learning the undesired subject could have been spent more efficiently, and with more lasting benefit, learning something else? No fact, concept, or subject needs to be known. If a pupil's interest in French wanes, he may profit by switching to a matter that concerns him. Contrary to the view of some educators that mastery is the only valid objective of language study, he may even benefit by jumping from language to language and gaining a smattering of each. Comparisons of languages, even at an elementary level, can provide learnings as valuable as the intensive learning of a single language.

This line of argument, however, avoids the issue. If a student must learn French for admission to college, he must learn French. Besides, shouldn't a pupil learn that there are certain requirements in life?

As for the second point, life certainly has its requirements. But if learning a foreign language is among them, it is for a most artificial reason—namely, a college entrance requirement. If life has its requirements, we need not worry that pupils will fail to learn this lesson. A requirement that is, relatively, a waste of time need not be placed in their path just to teach them this lesson.

Again, unfortunately, anger and ridicule, however valid, leave the requirement intact. Therefore, teachers at Potseloo do all they can to arouse an interest in a foreign language and to maintain it. They use records, tapes, and films. They turn to native-speaking helpers in the community. They relate the language to the people's culture, history, and international relations. They use the foreign language to teach aspects of various other subjects. They examine with some students the history of college entrance requirements in Western civilization and the arguments thought to justify them today.

Yet they are often forced to entice youngsters to learn beyond the point normally considered acceptable at Potseloo. The ultimate element in the seductive process is, of course, a threat: "If you don't learn enough French, you won't get into college. We are sorry, we think it is wrong, we are doing what we can to eliminate the requirement, but the requirement exists.''

Few upper-year students need much coaxing. If they wish to go to college, they face facts fully as well as do students in other schools.

Thus, even Potseloo must occasionally place requirements before education. For centuries, secondary schools in the Western world have humbly viewed themselves as doorsteps to those august institutions of learning to which we refer as higher. For centuries, secondary schools have sought less to bring out the potentials of students than to pump into students the knowledge required for candidacy to higher education. Worse yet, they have often assumed that these two goals were identical. In the United States, the dominance of the colleges eased somewhat as more and more of the non-college bound went to high school. Then the pendulum swung back, as more high school students recognized the college degree as conducive to advancement in life. A period of widespread unemployment of multiple-degree holders did little to stem the tide. Still, in the face of growing access by the disadvantaged to higher education and growing acceptability of applicants from unorthodox high schools, the traditional type of college-entrance requirements seemed unlikely to reassert its dominance.

Education, Mr. Chubb contends, is too important to leave to those who claim to know its proper content. "If our teachers tell you that a student loves to learn, that he thinks clearly, that he questions all things," he urges the college entrance authorities, "admit him without asking whether he knows U. S. History, French conversation, and even Ivanhoe or Silas Marner. You'll be lucky to have him."

THE TEACHER MISTOOK TWO CHILDREN'S LOCKER NUMBERS,
ONE LOW AND ONE HIGH, FOR THEIR RESPECTIVE IQ'S . . .
(See page 89).

THE TEACHERS' TIME PROBLEM

Mr. Chubb is often asked whether the Potseloo system does not place impossible demands on the teachers' time. Traditionally, a teacher conducts one curriculum at a time with an entire class. Must not the Potseloo teacher conduct 25 different activities simultaneously? Traditionally, a teacher can devote his main efforts during the school day to carrying out his plans. Must not the Potseloo teacher spend so much time during the day planning that he has little time to teach?

Mr. Chubb's first response is that he sees no choice. He repeats his usual question: is it not absurd to contend that the same 25 pupils just happen to be ready to spend the same 45 minutes each day going through the same (or even different) units of a physics course? In comparison with the progress each pupil might otherwise be making at that time, time is being wasted in colossal amounts.

84

The more practical part of Mr. Chubb's answer consists of reference to the help which pupils receive from other pupils and from citizens in the community. In particular, the drilling of skills and dispensing and explaining of knowledge can in large part be entrusted to books, language laboratories, teaching machines, specialists in the community, and pupils who help to teach. Also helpful is the fact that the time and staff traditionally devoted in a school system to general curriculum planning have been, in Potseloo, transferred to teaching. Therefore, teachers have time for planning and evaluating.

How much time and effort, in a more ordinary class, does the teacher spend enticing or requiring pupils to be interested in the work at hand? Teachers at Potseloo have their time and energy free for better pursuits, for pupils engaged in matters that truly interest them can work alone or with each other for considerable periods, particularly as they get older. More teachers at Potseloo have found it necessary to spend more time with each little child than was initially anticipated; correspondingly, they have needed to spend less time with older pupils. In traditional terms, the pupil-teacher ratio has had to be improved in the early grades, at the painless expense of the upper grades.

Still, teachers at Potseloo, like good teachers everywhere, do suffer from a shortage of time. They realize, however, that when the old course of action is intrinsically defective, it is worth the struggle to make an intrinsically superior course of action succeed.

CAN INCOMPETENT TEACHERS BE TRUSTED WITH SO MUCH DISCRETION?

The Potseloo system obviously demands that considerable confidence be reposed in each teacher. He must constantly make judgments as to what learning activity is best suited to a given pupil at a given moment. He is free to make any decisions which he believes will promote his pupils' progress toward the fundamental goals of the school.

Some educators and other citizens lack confidence in the ability of some, if not most, teachers to make wise decisions in a situation of virtually complete freedom. It is hard to say just which teachers are poor and which are good, particularly in view of the fact that some pupils flourish under a teacher whom other pupils deem incompetent. But let us disregard these complications for a moment and assume that a given teacher is indeed poor and that considerations such as tenure justify his retention.

86

Does it follow that he can be trusted in a rigid framework of restrictions, rules, and tests?

A poor teacher who has rules to observe, a syllabus to follow, and subject-matter goals to achieve may be able to keep his class busy and quiet. His pupils may wrap up the term in a neat package, labeled 80% or B, convincing the world that they have learned some history. But in the long term, most of the pupils have probably learned to dislike history, or at best they have wasted valuable time. They would probably have done better to spend the time chatting, swimming, or sleeping.

In short, however many restrictions and directions may surround a poor teacher, he retains and utilizes the freedom to teach poorly. At the same time, the framework is likely to inhibit the creative teacher from seizing—or even noticing—the opportunities for greater and more diversified development which every pupil often presents.

Conceivably, even a poor teacher would do better at Potseloo than in a straitjacket. Some human beings rise to a challenge when faith is shown in their ability to meet it. There is little to lose, and perhaps much to gain, by giving every teacher the opportunity to act like a professional.

A NEW VISION OF TEACHING

A prime factor in the ability to rise to the challenge of freedom is the desire to do so. Yet the belief is widespread, even among educators, that most teachers relish the security of knowing in detail what is expected of them and how they are expected to do it. Most teachers, it is said, refuse to take advantage of the rather broad freedom which is at their disposal in virtually any school. Mr. Chubb is able to find the type of faculty he needs only because the independent, bold few gravitate to the challenge of freedom which he offers. His system could not spread widely. So it is said.

Admittedly, teaching at Potseloo is not for the weak. Teachers there are daily impressed with the almost overwhelming significance of the goals they are pursuing, with the magnitude of their personal responsibility in the pursuit of those goals, with the necessity of constant learning that is thrust upon them.

But expectations, low or high, about people have a tendency to be self-fulfilling. Sam Shepard, Assistant Superintendent of the St. Louis Public Schools, tells the tale of a teacher who mistook two children's locker numbers, one low and one high, for their respective IQ's. She concluded, of course, that little could be expected of the one and much of the other. They quickly justified her expectations.

If the nature of the education system demanded independent, genuinely creative responses of teachers, not only would many appropriate people be attracted to the profession, but vast numbers of today's teachers might rise to the expectations. It would not be surprising if further studies confirm the finding that teachers who have had experience in guiding independent study typically want more of the same. *

Some teachers, having dug themselves deeper into the same rut for one or more decades, may truly lack the strength to climb out. But many, exposed for the first time to the demands of full professionalism, would recover from the initial shock and thrive in the new atmosphere.

What is needed is a new vision of teaching or, rather, a thorough-going implementation of John Dewey's expectation that teachers be "thoughtful

---

* Finding of William M. Alexander, Vynce A. Hines, Ernest Bentley, R. J. Moriconi, and James Wells in U. S. Office of Education Cooperative Research Project grant No. 2969. Reported in "Independent Study," *Curriculum Report of the National Association of Secondary School Principals,* May 1967, p. 8.

and independent." Teacher militancy should not be concerned solely with the role of teachers in decisions on salary and working conditions. It should not be directed at all toward securing a greater voice for teachers in the making of traditional curricular decisions. Rather, it should be dedicated to the replacement of traditional curriculum by liberated teaching. Teachers should have the courage to insist that, whatever the inadequacies of the science and theory of education today, and whatever their personal limitations, their personal best—without any planned frameworks—is by far the best that can be done for their pupils. And, by the standards of most education today, that is superb.

APPARENTLY THE UNDERLYING CONCERN OF
THE GHETTO ALL ALONG HAD BEEN FOR NOTHING MORE VICIOUS
THAN SELF-RESPECT AND GOOD EDUCATION . . .
(See page 124).

TEACHER STATUS

The prestige of the Potseloo teaching staff was initially high. Since then it has risen. The explanation lies in the nature of the job these teachers are called upon to do.

In traditional schools, the better teachers are those who succeed in adapting their segment of the curriculum to the greatest number of pupils in the class. To make most of the class digest the segment and benefit from it in any important sense—to convert the knowledge into interiorized action, as Piaget urges—is a Herculean task. To go further and expect that most of the pupils are spending most of their class time in the best way for each of them is to expect the impossible. (Unfortunately, in most schools teachers are not expected to trouble themselves with this latter concern.) Even where teachers have much flexibility to individualize within the limits of the subject matter, most of the difficulty remains, for it is fatuous to assume that all pupils in a group wisely spend the same pre-determined

92

amount of time on the same days of the week learning the same subject.

At Potseloo the situation is utterly different. Almost all the pupils want to learn what they are learning at any given moment. The teachers' task, in this respect, is far easier than that of most teachers. In addition, the teachers seek to ensure that the way each pupil is spending his time is the best way he can spend it, that it is helping him to progress toward objectives of life-long value. Therefore, the teachers' task is one in which to take pride.

At the same time, each teacher's task is supremely demanding. His range of options is not limited by any preconceived delimitation of the subject matter or by any set course of activities for entire groups. The content of his job is potentially infinite. Instead of knowing that the term will open with chapter one and close with a test, he rarely knows in advance the length of his dealings with any given pupil. Also, he must regularly admit his ignorance of subjects that arise, rather than appear perpetually as a knower.

In short, the fundamental job of most teachers is a difficult one, but for the wrong reasons. Teaching at Potseloo is at least as difficult, but for the right reasons. To point this out to the community is one of Mr. Chubb's favorite tasks.

In the course of their preparation for teaching, most students learn that teaching must be appropriate to each individual learner. Potseloo is one of the few schools which gives the teacher a fighting chance to do just that. At the same time, it is a school in which all teaching is directed toward specific, articulated ends. Some schools which are equally intent on individualizing instruction give the impression of letting the pupils run wild, to no set purpose, in the blind faith that the pupils' spontaneous interests will inevitably lead to good results. The combination of flexibility in choice of method and precision in choice of objective attracts many teachers to Potseloo and sustains the respect of the community.

Recruitment of excellent personnel has remained as simple each year as it was at the outset. Applications pour in from new college graduates and from experienced teachers, including a striking proportion of men. Women who are merely awaiting the right man seek out niches more comfortable than Potseloo. It is generally recognized that teaching at Potseloo is a job for the best minds.

In many parts of the United States, one commonly hears that the brightest college students would be ill advised to waste their capacities as public school teachers. This disparagement has always seemed blasphemous to educators, in view of the overwhelming importance of the development of our young people's capacities, and in view of the inherent majesty of a profession dedicated to that development. But pleas for higher status for teachers have fallen on deaf ears. Potseloo has found a method that works much better than pleading: it has made the job of the teacher irresistibly worthy of respect.

POTSELOO AND
THE DISADVANTAGED

Most of the teachers at Potseloo had faith that their concept of education was inherently applicable to all children. In fact, some held that no children stood to lose more from an ordinary curriculum than disadvantaged children, whatever enrichment, compensation, head start, and extra staff might be grafted on for their benefit. Some slum children, they recognized, are attuned to various types of captivity— poverty, self-contempt, meagerness of experience, family instability, constant fatigue. But they are not prepared for the type of captivity traditionally demanded in school. For most children, the Potseloo teachers argued, instruction that is not totally individualized is merely colossally inefficient. For slum children it is a tragedy of the first magnitude, virtually condemning them to personal misery and to reproduction of their misery.

For over a decade, however, the teachers were not in a position to base their boasts on experience. Potseloo was an all-white and for the most part well-educated, comfortable suburb.

When the school was embarking on its twelfth year of life, and a first class was about to graduate, the school board considered the establishment of a kindergarten the following September. Five-year-olds would be able to come to school if their parents so desired. Support for a kindergarten had been growing for years, but it did not overcome taxpayers' opposition until the need for adding a grade to the school each year had passed.

Meanwhile, voices from within and without the community were urging the admission of some disadvantaged children, most of whom were Negro, from Letlit. Civil rights organizations were pressing the suburbs to desegregate their housing and their schools. Educators from other communities, well meaning or otherwise, were challenging Mr. Chubb to try his system on a new breed of youngsters. And the state legislature, disregarding school district boundaries, was considering the withholding of state funds from schools that were almost totally white but that were situated within ten miles of largely Negro schools.

Within Potseloo itself, some parents feared that the admission of Negroes would lower the scholastic and moral level of the school and would lead to racial friction. Some of them were repelled by the rising incidence of crime and rioting in Letlit's ghetto area. Others viewed as baseless the fear that, in a school where pupils were not expected to keep in step with each other, scholastic standards would be affected by the admission of disadvantaged pupils. They attributed the violence in Letlit to the frustrations of ghetto life in the midst of affluence and to the frustration of being a Negro in the United States. They considered it their duty to foster the unity of American society, or to forestall what they viewed as a trend toward irreparable disunity. Many wished to give less fortunate children a chance to attend school in happier circumstances. Some parents feared that their own children were missing an opportunity to acquaint themselves with their multiracial society. Teachers, in addition to sharing these motivations, wanted to investigate (or display) the breadth of applicability of the Potseloo method.

Another factor conducive to admission of disadvantaged children was the fact that, until recently, many Potseloo families had had children in mixed schools in Letlit. Parents with experience of integration tended to be less fearful of integration than were other parents. Finally, some parents were motivated by the calculation that a desegration process planned and controlled by the local school board was preferable to one directed by the state capital or other "outside" forces.

Most Potseloo teachers and parents believed that an early start was of the utmost importance for disadvantaged children. The wisest course, they felt, was to establish school facilities for four-year-olds and to admit disadvantaged children to them, delaying the inauguration of a kindergarten until the following year. There was widespread agreement, however, that local four-year-olds were also ready for a variety of experiences that their homes could not provide them.

The following September, ten four-year-olds each morning and ten each afternoon were bussed from Letlit to Potseloo, where they attended school with local four-year-olds. The program was varied. The two teachers spent considerable time with the pupils' parents, both at school and, whenever possible, at the children's homes. They tried to introduce the children and their parents to a wealth of new experiences and to follow up on all interests which the children displayed. Problems of undernourishment, fatigue, and poor teeth, hearing, or vision were attacked both directly and by helping the parents to help their children.

Thus, the nursery program at Potseloo resembled that of most good schools. The real difference began two years later when, by agreement with the Letlit school board, the Letlit children who so desired remained at Potseloo.

Most of the Negro pupils have matured academically with each passing year. Their self-confidence and high motivation have persisted. They remain confident and motivated at Potseloo for the same reason as other children: they sense that every teacher respects their interests, and hence respects them as human beings. Many regularly demonstrate to themselves that they can learn as well as anyone else. They are not required to choose between learning what others command them to learn and failing; rather, they are helped to learn about matters that genuinely interest them.

The teachers believe that another reason for this success is the relatively early start of all the disadvantaged children at Potseloo. Because of their youth, and because they had not yet learned the American lesson that black is shameful, their minds were still malleable. The school was able to help them develop pride in themselves as human beings even if their parents did not know how to teach them pride in themselves as Negroes.

In addition, as indicated in the 1966 U. S. Office of Education study, *Equality of Educational Opportunity,* attendance at school with children of a more favored social and economic background helps disadvantaged children to develop faith in their ability to influence their future.

However, some of the fundamental educational difficulties of disadvantaged Negroes have not vanished at Potseloo. A higher percentage of Negro than of white pupils lag in development of their abilities of abstract reasoning—questioning, understanding the meaning of data, verifying, recognizing premises and consequences.

The lagging children appear to be the most deprived. Most of them, the teachers believe, have suffered *in utero* or in the first years of life from malnutrition. Their parents were probably the least able to offer intellectual stimulation as well.

Even these children probably progress further and suffer less at Potseloo than they would in Letlit's ghetto schools. But Potseloo's impact, having been delayed until the children reached the ripe old age of four, has come too late in their lives to achieve truly gratifying success.

It is not only the children bussed in from Letlit who have benefitted at Potseloo. Limiting one's contacts to black or white Americans, or to rich or poor Americans, would seem a poor way to expand one's understanding of the world. Yet, in the beginning, some parents in Potseloo considered personal acquaintance with disadvantaged children to be about as desirable as personal experience with disease. This view lost adherents with time, for most pupils seemed to be developing a healthy, respectful attitude toward each other.

The secret appears to lie not just in the academic success of many of the Negro pupils, but in the success of teachers in promoting true communication among pupils as well. The presence of different cultures has been exploited in class to promote awareness in each pupil of his own values and of American ideals and reality. True communication has not always been easy to achieve or comfortable to experience. But most pupils emerge from the experience with much deeper knowledge of themselves and of others. They develop a healthy respect for the impact of environment on all they are as individuals.

And some of them become painfully aware of a discrepancy between the ideals which their country—and perhaps their family—professes and the values which it lives.

American educators underwent in 1954 the humiliation of having to be told by the judicial system what they, more than anyone else, should have known: that segregated education is inherently inferior. Potseloo's educators believe that racially or culturally separate education is inferior for all pupils. They are not waiting for the judges or legislators to force them to act on this belief. Nor are they prepared to tolerate and hence promote the mutual ignorance in which racial contempt and racial hatred fester.

Awareness—deep awareness—that "race" has much less meaning than "human being," and that all human beings desperately need self-respect, is a common component of the "knowledge of the world" that Potseloo's students now achieve. Since it is knowledge, it lends itself to being distilled into a unit or even a course. It may some day become a required subject in many schools.

Heaven forbid!

ANARCHY OF THE SORT
THAT OCCURS WHEN EACH HUMAN BEING BREATHES
THE AIR ADJACENT TO HIS OWN NOSE . . .
(See page 129).

CHAPTER □ IV

In the ghetto

New Amsterdam is utterly different from Potseloo. It teems with people. Its air is foul. It lacks greenery and tranquility. Its automobiles stand still. Its crime rate leaps ahead. Its municipal employees, in unhesitant contempt for the law, regularly plague the city with strikes. Its schools oscillate with growing speed from crisis to crisis.

Yet one school district in New Amsterdam, in the heart of the Negro ghetto, has much in common with Potseloo.

... AND HE BECAME A LITTLE CHILD

—William Blake

Few passers-by perceived in Rick Smith's violence, apathy, or arrogance a desperate, doomed desire to believe in himself.

Public School 362 had deepened Rick's sense of worthlessness and futility. There he had spent parts of eight years perfecting his ability to fail—there, where cops in the halls maintained security, where the bio lab could collect its rats from the halls, where junkies hung around trying to make a convert or a sale. There he was told every day, a hundred times, now subtly, now bluntly, that he was wrong—wrong in the way he thought, wrong in the way he talked, wrong in the way he dressed, wrong in the type of family he came from, wrong in the type of house he lived in.

Now, Rick and his friends took great joy in shattering the school's windows. Eventually, the district superintendent and school board decided that the only adequate response to the siege was to strengthen the fortress. All the windows of P.S. 362 were bricked up over the summer, and air conditioning had to be installed. The money thus spent could have been better used to improve education, but war is war.

P.S. 362 is the fortress in which John Smith, Rick's youngest brother, is enrolled. He has a brother in the second grade and a half-sister in the seventh, but he is the first in his family to attend nursery school.

John knows intuitively that Mrs. Wiener is his friend. She is one of those rare people who is all but overwhelmed when a child loves her, for she believes that there is nothing purer, nothing freer of ulterior motives, than the love of a child. Children can distinguish genuine respect from a facade of politeness or condescension, and Mrs. Wiener genuinely respects her charges.

Mrs. Wiener is white and Jewish, and short and dumpy. John Smith is too young for any of these facts to matter to him, but the warmth of the relationship is planting seeds that will blossom forth in later years. Mrs. Wiener is John's first real contact with authority. How different from Rick's contacts and from many which John himself, as a Negro, will have later on! Because of Mrs. Wiener, John will be predisposed to seeing school and society as friendly. It will be harder for him than it was for Rick to learn to despise whites, or Negroes, or himself. He may even be kindly disposed from now on toward people who are short and dumpy.

If John gets nothing else out of nursery school, Mrs. Wiener will have earned her keep many times over.

Mrs. Wiener came to P.S. 362 on the heels of a frightful storm—a storm that raged for a full two years and virtually tore the city and its educational system apart.

THE PEDIATRICIAN AND THE SCHOOLS

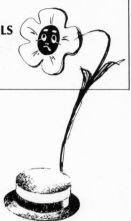

For decades the city had seen minority groups rise up out of the depths of its poverty and move on to positions of honor in American life. Now the depths were occupied by Negroes, who differed in a vital way from all the minorities that had preceded them. They were the first to lack, not just a position of honor in American life, but a reliable sense of self-respect as well. The Poles, the Italians, the Jews, and the Irish had, in the hallowed American tradition, been held in as much contempt; but the proud cultures which their parents instilled in them had generally immunized them against self-contempt. Men have a dishonest, saving tendency to take personal pride in accomplishments to which they personally have made not the slightest contribution.

If Negroes, on the other hand, had much to be proud of, few of them knew it. In music and sports—areas in which they were respected even if long discriminated against—they proved their worth. Otherwise, being held in contempt, they tended to hold themselves in contempt, and therefore lacked the strength to lift themselves up.

Many citizens recognized that the plight of the Negroes was more desperate than the plight of any earlier minority. Many feared the growing militancy and tendency toward civil disorder among Negroes. Many criticized the schools for failing to reach slum children. For these reasons, the climate was propitious for acceptance of an increasingly vociferous demand from ghetto leaders that school control be decentralized. The central office on East Street agreed to delegate much of its authority, on an experimental basis, to the hitherto virtually powerless local board of the Drainer District, the heart of the ghetto.

Decentralization precipitated bitter competition for positions on the local board. For the first time, a school board election in the Drainer District attracted genuine public interest.

Militant black radicals won three of the five positions on the new board. Its first act, one month before the school year opened, was to declare that it would not accept a single white teacher or principal who had planned to continue working in the district.

The battle was joined. The local board cited what it termed the demonstrated inability of white teachers and principals to do the pupils any good. The city and state teacher organizations were hardly convinced. The central office claimed final power over all placement matters, and firmly rejected the concept of placement based on race alone.

In the subsequent test of passions and wills, most of the teachers throughout the city went on strike. Many black and most white teachers viewed the dispute primarily as one of job security; militant leaders on both sides viewed it primarily as a ladder to personal power. Racial hatreds solidified.

Then Dr. Hanes stepped in, gently and with overwhelming effect.

Dr. Horatio Hanes, an Arkansas sharecropper's son who had made good, was a pediatrician. On the staff of Children's Hospital, in the center of the ghetto, he treated children in the public wards. Other than in his medical work, he had never shown much interest in the problems of black America. But one phenomenon intrigued him. For years, even before the first riots, the nights had vibrated to the shattering of glass at P.S. 362 on the hill just above the hospital; yet the hospital had never been attacked.

As the educational and racial situation deteriorated, Dr. Hanes conceived the idea of exploiting the respect which the hospital enjoyed in an effort to reverse the current and bind up the community's wounds. He decided to run for the school board of the Drainer District.

The election changed the complexion of the Board. Dr. Hanes was elected handily over a militant incumbent. Desperate for a way out of the educational impasse, the board chose him, a novice, as its chairman.

During the campaign, Dr. Hanes had made clear his concern for the rights of teachers. But he had insisted that the public must place first things first:

a school exists to educate children. No one who hinders the ability of a school to fulfill this function should be retained in that school.

After the election, the new board proposed to the city board that all of the district's teachers and principals who felt that they could do a professional job in the district be invited to return. Subsequently, those who proved unable to meet the challenge would be expected to request a transfer. The local superintendent would be responsible for recommending qualified individuals to fill any vacancies.

The local board contended that, in disputed cases, equitable means existed for ruling on teachers' success. Experience itself would disclose which teachers had most problems of discipline; which teachers best developed the pupils' self-esteem; which teachers made pupils want most to learn; which teachers felt a genuine sense of accomplishment. Principals and the local superintendent would have to spend more time assessing teacher success than ever before.

The criteria, of course, were easier to state than to apply. And in assessing principals, the only criterion in disputed cases was to be the judgment of the superintendent. The plan could therefore give rise to serious difficulties. But it promised a respite from turmoil, a renewal of the educational process— perhaps even a narrowing of the gulf between the races. The central office on East Street agreed to a two-year trial.

By this time, over half the former teachers in the district were working elsewhere and had no desire to return. The vacancies were filled by rash college graduates and experienced teachers from other districts (like Mrs. Wiener) who were motivated by the desire for adventure or for work that they deemed of true significance. In its employment policies the board was careful not to discriminate racially; but it did give preference to men over women, in recognition of the absence of fathers in many households.

It quickly became apparent that, the younger the children he taught, the more likely a teacher was to feel—and to have reason to feel—successful. The older the children, the more necessary it became to refine the concept of "the successful teacher," speaking instead of "the teacher successful with certain children and unsuccessful with others." If all pupils were to have an opportunity to succeed, frequent pupil transfers would be necessary until the right combination was found. But the number of teachers of each grade or subject was obviously limited. Moreover, it was impractical to subject pupils and teachers to frequent interruptions of their progress through the curriculum.

In short, it appeared that the local board, despite the powers it had acquired, would be forced to leave many children in an inadequate educational situation. It would not be possible to find the right pupil-teacher combination for getting every pupil through the curriculum.

AN IDEA

During lunch one day, Mr. Ganley, the principal of Bardun Senior High School in the Drainer District, overheard a conversation between two of his teachers. They were discussing the report, which one of them had read in a professional journal, of a dispute between Negro and white students at a high school in Connecticut. Negro history had recently been introduced into the history curriculum. The Negroes contended that there was still inadequate emphasis on the subject, while the whites claimed that it was overstressed.

"Why can't they let the Negroes study more Negro history and the whites study less?" asked one of the teachers.

The other objected to the suggestion. "The purpose of teaching Negro history is to teach respect for Negroes. Either this is good for everyone or it is not.

112

Besides, are they all Americans or not? Once you start encroaching on the common experiences that pupils have in our public schools, what will happen to the unity that's left in this country? If the study of a subject as basic as history is to have a different content for different races, you're moving back toward segregation. And another thing: suppose not all the Negro students agree on how much Negro history they want to learn? Once you start letting pupils decide for themselves how much they'll learn of different subjects, you'll have chaos, and probably very little learning. What would happen if my pupils could decide that they are not interested in English literature, or that they want to concentrate on pornography?''

"Look," replied the first teacher. "We have electives, don't we? We don't make everyone learn the same things."

"That's it! That's it!" Mr. Ganley exclaimed. "That's what?" asked the teachers. But the principal was already on his way to his office to call the local superintendent.

Two weeks later, East Street was pondering a request from the Drainer District school board for another exemption from regulations. Dr. Hanes proposed that the District's schools be freed of all year-by-year subject-matter requirements, effective the following September. "If we had an unlimited supply of teachers and time, each pupil would eventually find someone who could teach each required subject adequately," Dr. Hanes wrote. "Short of this, we know of no way to help each student learn to the best of his ability, other than to find out the things he is genuinely motivated to learn and then help him to learn them, even if, as a result, he will not hear about the Pilgrims or refraction all year."

In the year since its election, the Drainer school board had restored the educational process and a measure of tranquility to the community. This was no time to show lack of confidence in Dr. Hanes. East Street approved his request.

The teachers were informed that, while they were henceforth free of all subject-matter require-ments, they were at liberty to continue teaching as before if they thought this to be in their pupils' best interests. The local board and superintendent recommended, however, that each teacher, from September on, direct his efforts at helping each pupil learn what he could most profitably be learning at any given time. The board and superintendent recognized, as they wrote to the teachers, that "this system may prove excessively demanding of your time, or otherwise unworkable. However, in theory at least, it seems an utterly natural system, particularly for children whose greatest educational problem is the lack of motivation to learn what they are told to learn. We therefore hope that you will join us in trying to make the system work."

The Drainer District still needed to clarify its goals further. With love of learning as its only con-scious goal, it lacked much of the basis which Potse-loo gave to its teachers for guiding learning toward definite ends. But it had recognized that education must defer, if any healthy learning was to take place, to the individual's need to respect himself. It had recognized, in other words, the absurdity of failing to respect each pupil's genuine motivations—the absurdity of much that it had hitherto done.

For John Smith in his nursery class, things were probably not much different under the new system than they would have been under the old. Mrs. Wiener was in either case free to tell stories to the children; to give them a kind feeling about books; to broaden their acquaintance with the world; to improve the ways they worked and played together; and to help them tie their shoelaces or blow their noses. Very little children are genuinely happy, she found, to follow each of the thousand paths along which a teacher may guide them. In most cases, an activity suggested to them is just as genuinely what they want to do as almost any other activity would be. All that is necessary is that they feel secure and warm with the teacher.

But the new system meant a world of difference to John's brother Lenny.

BEAUTY AND THE BUG

Lenny was in the second grade, in Miss Evans' class. He had had trouble with reading the previous year, but the teacher had, of necessity, obliged him to keep at it. Over the summer, Lenny lost the meager reading ability which he had managed to acquire in the first grade; but the summer left intact the hearty dislike for reading with which the first grade had endowed him.

Miss Evans, however, was able to afford a convalescent period for Lenny. She was under no obligation to raise him to second-grade reading level by June. Rather, she had time to ferret out his interests and help him to learn on the basis of them, meanwhile subtly demonstrating to him the value of books.

She quickly learned that Lenny had a genuine interest in—unfortunately—bugs. She asked him if he could catch some in bottles and bring them into class. This was an act of self-abnegation approaching heroism, for Miss Evans had almost as deep an aversion to insects as toward the rat she feared she would see any day in class or in the hall. But within a few weeks, both she and Lenny had acquired a wealth of information about bugs. Some of it came from research in the library at night, the results of which she communicated to Lenny the next day. Lenny's other sources of information were experience (for instance, he failed to punch holes in the caps of the bottles containing his first specimens), close observation, and a few brief but treasured meetings with the seventh-grade biology teacher.

In December, Miss Evans gave up her search for a reading primer that dealt with, or at least mentioned, bugs. Instead, she borrowed for two days a fifth-grade volunteer who wrote down, in his best printing, what Lenny told him about bugs. The day before Christmas vacation began, the fifth-grader presented the "book" to Lenny as a present, and Miss Evans told Lenny that, in reality, *he* was the author of the book.

By January 3, upon returning from vacation, Lenny was able to read some of "his" book. A boy who had hated the thought of reading had now spent a vacation learning to decipher words like "cockroach." Suddenly, bugs had a certain beauty to Miss Evans.

Meanwhile, she was striving to provide individual curriculums to 27 other children as well. At the beginning of the year, her efforts were almost superhuman. Lack of assistance, lack of books at the primer level on most of the subjects in which she needed them, and the hostility or fear of some children toward the educational process hampered her at every turn.

Gradually she learned time-saving devices, like that of enlisting the help of an upper-grader to print Lenny's book or to teach individual second-graders things they wanted to know. As one would suspect, these devices often spread the benefits at least as much as they spread the burden. That is why the upper-grade teachers were eager to oblige her requests for pupils.

Eventually, Miss Evans realized how little time she was spending disciplining children who were bored with what they were doing. She began to realize how much time she had spent in previous years just trying to hold children's attention. Now, many of her second-graders were beginning to learn by themselves for appreciable spans of time and to rely somewhat less on her for encouragement, verification, and guidance.

Miss Evans derived considerable gratification also from her frequent excursions into areas of knowledge that were new to her. These excursions aggravated her time problem; but she could not recall a year in which she had learned nearly so much.

Most important, she had never before felt so keenly that all her efforts were worthwhile. More than ever before she beheld the joy of sudden understanding light up her children's faces. More than ever before she was convinced that her children were learning to love learning.

THEORY MEETS PRACTICE

The results of the new system were more disparate and less often gratifying in Mr. Cellini's seventh grade. Greta Smith, the eldest half-sister of John and Lenny, had already begun the decline in measured IQ which sets in for so many slum children during their school years. Her reading level was almost respectable—5.2—at the end of the sixth grade, which placed her in the upper third of her class. But for her, as for most of the seventh-graders, school was at best something to suffer stoically until one reached the age of 17.

Mr. Cellini, a new teacher, had been deeply impressed in his education courses with the virtues of individualized instruction. He eagerly accepted the freedom from curricular restraints which the Drainer District had acquired. Thus, he began the school year by asking the students to write a one- or two-page composition on a subject of their choice. He would correct their mistakes, he said, so that they could improve their writing; but he would grade the compositions solely in accordance with the amount of interest in the subject which they seemed to reveal.

The interests expressed in the compositions fell into several categories. Having learned in his recently completed teacher education the virtues of participation by pupils in the decisions which affect them, he listed the subjects on the blackboard and asked how the students interested in each could learn more about it. Since no teacher had ever before relied in this way on their advice, many pupils assumed that the exercise lacked sincerity, and they treated it with derision. Mr. Cellini made the additional mistake of choosing "pretty clothes" as the first subject for ideas; mockery from the "tough guys" in the class forced him to call off the exercise after five or ten minutes of futility.

Falling back on his own ideas, Mr. Cellini decided, among other things, to introduce Greta (through her interest in pretty clothes) to the history of fashion, and thus to history itself. Several months of effort revealed to him, however, that her sole motivation in the area of pretty clothes was to sew them.

Many of the boys drove him into an even deeper impasse. After a time they recognized that the teacher's wish to have them engage in learning activities which genuinely interested them was sincere. They then proceeded to take "advantage" of this novel circumstance by trying to get away with as little learning as possible.

In his more optimistic moments, Mr. Cellini reasoned that, despite appearances to the contrary, the same boys in a more structured curriculum would probably be learning no more than they were now. Indeed, hadn't the measured IQ's of many of them been declining since the third grade? Perhaps he had arrested the decline, and if so, hadn't he done better than their teachers in previous years?

Mr. Cellini was too honest a man to be sustained for long by this reasoning. Perhaps his pupils' IQ's were continuing to decline. Besides, an institution without positive accomplishments hardly merits public support. At times, Mr. Cellini was sorely tempted to use the powerful frame that had served him well on the college football field to knock some sense into his pupils' heads.

Driven by a combination of despair and renewed determination, he spent four days of his Christmas vacation visiting the parents of his more difficult pupils. In part, his motivation was to reap the rewards which, according to one of his education professors, would flow from a display to parents of interest in their children. In part, he hoped to derive general information and specific ideas that would suggest his next steps in class.

He came away from these meetings with a better understanding of some of the children and a few helpful leads on specific activities. But on January 3 he arrived at school as perplexed as ever on approaches to most of his difficult pupils. Most of them remained as unfathomable as he had always found them. Greta, for example, still looked upon him as

121

she would look upon another life form, as if his efforts had no connection with anything that her life was or would be.

Did his failures stem solely from a personal incompetence to meet the challenge he had so eagerly sought the previous summer? Talks with his fellow seventh- and eighth-grade teachers saved Mr. Cellini from this frightening conclusion. He found that his colleagues, too, were afflicted by an inability to reach most of their students. They, too, wondered at times whether to ask for a transfer before being asked to transfer.

They recognized that they were working at a disadvantage as compared to teachers in the lower grades. The lesson that school is irrelevant or frightening had had more time to ingrain itself in older pupils. But, certainly, a capacity for intellectual progress lurked somewhere in every student. Where was the key to finding it?

They knew that there was no quick, certain, or universally applicable way to cure a deep contempt for self or fear of school. The illness had been long neglected and would require a long convalescence. The best they could do was to persist in the search for ways to unlock the promise in each student.

They decided to enlist all the help they could find in the community—mothers who would serve as aides, men who would talk to interested pupils about their careers, college students who would tutor. Dr. Hanes was an early volunteer. He offered to bring interested students to the hospital, where he would demonstrate and explain to them his work and that of the laboratories. Some students found the visit so intriguing that, in collaboration with their teachers, Dr. Hanes soon had to plan further visits and readings for them.

In Greta's case, too, there was a breakthrough. By March, to her own amazement, she was displaying genuine promise in painting. The art teacher found a potter downtown who was happy to display her works. To Greta's still greater amazement, two of them were purchased. They were portraits of the assassinated leaders John F. Kennedy and Martin Luther King. This success revolutionized her attitude toward school. No longer so doubtful of herself, she became more outgoing and wanted to please her teachers. Mr. Cellini was even more impressed by the observation that her new self-esteem was hardly tinged by arrogance or conceit. He marveled that a girl who previously had known so little success could possess such beauty of character. His deepened respect for Greta reinforced her developing conviction that school might be worthwhile after all.

Of course, such very happy endings—or beginnings—were rare. But there were good signs of a more general nature. In particular, attendance was excellent in the last few months of the school year. Apparently the hitherto deepening hostility of the pupils toward school had been reversed in most cases, and every student had at least one or two experiences of successful learning. The teachers next September would, therefore, have a better chance to succeed.

RAYS OF SUNSHINE

The effect of the new method on the community was dramatic. Demands in the ghetto for totally decentralized control, for a virtual divorce of the Drainer District from the central office on East Street, became less strident in the face of the evident movement toward control of the educational process by the pupils themselves and by the teachers who knew them best. The criticism that pupils were not learning enough remained frequent, but even the most militant leaders agreed that, at least in the Drainer District schools, "honky" was no longer ruining black children. Apparently the underlying concern of the ghetto all along had been for nothing more vicious than self-respect and good education.

Meanwhile, the white population of the city, reassured by the physical calm in the ghetto and by the respect for teachers' rights there, began to express liberal views again. The school board seized the opportunity presented by these new attitudes to ask parents throughout the city to volunteer their services to the Drainer schools as tutors, aides, or introducers of their lines of work. The number of ghetto residents who had valuable services to offer surprised many people, particularly in the ghetto itself. A pattern of community interning developed, with local residents, many of them without college degrees, sharing the teaching chores.

Dr. Hanes spoke for almost all Drainer District teachers when he predicted, at a year-end press conference, that the school situation would continue to improve. It just might be, he said, that children who start off at age four in a school whose sole objective is to bring out the best in them, rather than to force a traditional curriculum into them, would approach learning as a joy all their lives. In the eighth grade, and in all the years thereafter, they would, he hoped, be as susceptible to learning as they were in kindergarten, thus reversing the tradition of slum schools. "If we can do that," he said, "school will no longer seem irrelevant to thousands of pupils, and we will no longer be wasting the taxpayers' money.

"More important," he concluded, "we'll put an end to some of the most horrid cruelties of man to man—a mind that never develops, a person who goes through life without ever having a sense that he is worth something."

Admittedly, the story of P.S. 362 is not a totally happy one, particularly for the older children. For the senior high school, the story would include an even higher proportion of apparently unrewarded efforts by teachers. There may continue to be ample cause for concern even after many years of experience with the new system. Perhaps a person who suffers in infancy from malnutrition and severe intellectual deprivation is stunted for life, regardless of the efforts subsequently lavished upon him in school. It may be that P.S. 362 has arrived on the scene too late even for John Smith or some of his classmates in nursery school.

But better late than still later. The end result will probably be far better if a child begins enjoying an improved diet and intellectual stimuli at age four than at age five or six, if he begins by learning self-esteem rather than self-hatred, by learning the joy of knowing rather than the fear of trying. To learn these things is infinitely more vital than to learn, for regurgitation's sake, whatever else one may be told to learn.

John will still return home each evening to a brother consumed with hatred for the world and for himself. John may never walk an American street certain that he is viewed with the same respect as a man in a lighter wrapping.

But his first impression of life outside his home is that the sun shines as brightly on him as on anyone else.

WE HAVE NOT YET BEGUN TO DREAM OF MOST THINGS
WHICH MAN WILL HAVE DONE
IN THE FULL COURSE OF HIS HISTORY . . .
(See page 131).

All about the future   CHAPTER ☐ V

"What is essential in creating a learning environment in the classroom is freedom for the child—freedom of inquiry, freedom of expression, freedom from fear of being wrong.—John Holt at Conference of National Committee for Support of the Public Schools, April 1967. Quoted in NCSPS Newsletter, *May 1967.*

Obviously, no one has the time, during the course of his schooling or even of his lifetime, to learn what he really ought to know. This has long been the case. Today's knowledge explosion does not create a new problem; it only complicates a situation that, though we have not always recognized it as such, has long been hopeless. Still, the schools go on seeking the best possible combination of subject smatterings. Good schools perpetually revamp each smattering, the list of smatterings, and efforts to link the smatterings. The curriculum that results at any given moment is likely to be a compromise based

127

on honest educational considerations, the power of the factions behind the respective smatterings, the inertia of tradition, college entrance requirements, the demands of accrediting agencies, state law, and the availability of teachers and materials. Many of the pupils subjected to the curriculum learn some things well, and virtually all the pupils learn many things poorly and to no long avail. On subjects that have proven distasteful, many pupils decide that, if it is up to them (and in the final analysis it is), they will never bother to remedy their ignorance in the given areas.

Some of the poor results are due to poor teaching or to poorly constituted smatterings. But the problem goes much deeper. Even with universally good teaching and universally excellent choice of content of courses, the problem would be devastating. The basic defect is not in the carrying out of the system; the basic defect is the system itself. People just will not fit efficiently into the curricular molds which we in our wisdom—even our loving wisdom—plan for them.

I believe we must recognize that Herbert Spencer's question "What knowledge is of most worth?" is no longer the right question, and perhaps never was. Not only is the knowledge that is of great worth to people too vast for them ever to acquire, but the knowledge that is likely to be of great worth to a given individual in the circumstances of his particular life is largely unforseeable. Besides, if education the world over has taught us anything, it is this: that schools dedicated to the transmission of knowledge pay little genuine attention to the other ends which they claim to pursue, nor do they transmit knowledge to most students with impressive effect.

Rather than wonder what knowledge is of most worth, let us wonder what each individual pupil can do today that will matter to him while he does it and that stands a good chance of still mattering to him fifty years hence.

The first part of the question suggests its own answer: we must place the curricular problem fully in the lap of the teachers and their pupils. The only people who have a chance to sense what makes sense for an individual pupil at a given moment are the pupil himself and those adults who know him and who are with him.

Is this educational anarchy? Perhaps. But it is the anarchy that nature demands. It is anarchy of the sort that occurs when each human being breathes the air adjacent to his own nose. The analogy is not far-fetched. Were we to insist that a person draw air from a predetermined place, we would risk suffocating him. By insisting that each pupil partake of a curriculum planned for pupils in general, how many children do we suffocate every day?

The second part of the question—what will still matter to today's pupil when he is half a century older—does not suggest its own answer. It requires a knowledge of the future.

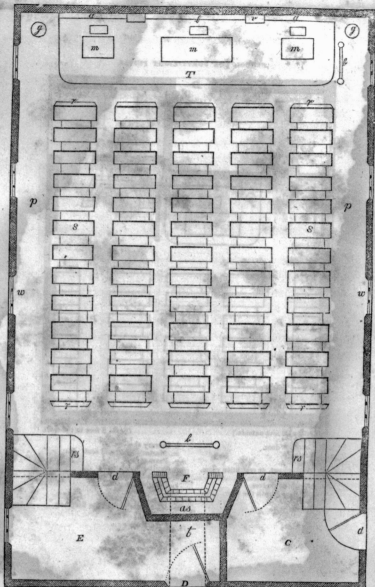

51 feet by 31 feet outside.]   [Scale 8 feet to the inch.

D. Entrance door.   E. Entry.   F. Fireplace.   C. Wood closet.   T. Teacher's platform.   a. Apparatus shelves.   t. Air tube beneath the floor.   d. Doors.   g. Globes.   l. Library shelves.   m. Master's table and seat.   p. Passages.   r. Recitation seats.   s. Scholars' desks and seats.   r s. Stairs to recitation rooms in the attic.   v. Ventilator.   w. Windows.   b. Movable blackboard.   a s. Air space behind the fireplace.

THE SCHOOL: Its objects, relations and uses *by Alonzo Potter—1843*
(Horace Mann, Secretary of the Board of Education)

HOW MUCH OF OUR TIME IN SCHOOL
WAS JUST PLAIN WASTED? . . .
(See page 157).

YESTERDAY AND TOMORROW

History is a field at least as dismal as any other. It is filled with such blunder, bluster, cruelty, and incompetence that it would seem to be a tale told of idiots. True, it recounts many triumphs of creativity and discovery. But how small these triumphs appear when viewed against the mediocrity, the horrors, the needs, and still more, the prospects!

In consideration of man's newfound capacity to change life at a pace some call rapid and some insane, a disconcerting prediction is probably in order: we have not even begun to dream of most of the things which man will have done in the full course of his history. We may, of course, destroy civilization one of these days. But if we do not, if we have the wisdom to limit ourselves, in the future as in the past, to mere retail fratricide, our species will probably achieve wonders that we are incapable today of imagining. Man's imagination is limited, after all, by the poverty of his history.

This prediction does little more than deny the possibility of predicting. It is really an anti-prediction. It must therefore be unsatisfactory to educators, who, like investors and weathermen, need a more specific picture of the morrow. All men are curious to peer into the future; educators, investors, and weathermen are forced to try. If educators rest assured, they must do so in the belief that the knowledge, skills, and characteristics which pupils are acquiring today will be useful to them beyond today. But educators must assume something further, and something even more difficult to justify: namely, that the things children are learning today will be more relevant tomorrow than all the other things that they could be learning today. Obviously, these assumptions must rest on some idea, whether articulated or not, of what tomorrow will bring.

My idea of tomorrow, however lacking in content, is full of practical potential. If it is right, it fundamentally challenges the wisdom of continuing to do anything that we do today in our schools. It says that there is little reason, unless evidence is supplied, to see a guide for the future of education in anything educators have done or now do with students. To say that man has not begun to dream of most of what he is yet to do, and to say further that the tempo of change is accelerating, is to see a widening chasm between ourselves and our past. It is ever less wise to present the wisdom of the fathers as a guide for the sons.

Yet how difficult it is to break—or even perceive —the shackles of past and present! How difficult to disenthrall ourselves of tradition! Tradition becomes habitual, like smoking. Besides, tradition often achieves the aura of common sense. One does not easily question common sense. But why not? Wasn't it common sense that the earth is the center of the universe? Wasn't it common sense that a given distance or a given period of time is an absolute under any condition? Wasn't it common sense that a different religion was a sacrilege and therefore a justification for holy war? Wasn't it common sense that some men are born to rule and others to be slaves? Wasn't it common sense that each man should be educated according to his station in life? Wasn't it common sense that to memorize something is to know it? Wasn't it common sense that what teachers teach is more or less what pupils learn? With such examples of extraordinary nonsense, once called common sense, is history strewn!

To overcome such traditions (and it would be as groundless to assume, without evidence, that traditions are wrong as to assume that they are right) has usually taken centuries of experience to the contrary. But perhaps, when it comes to the common sense that adults can say what youngsters should learn and when, one good healthy jolt could turn the trick. I do not claim the power to administer such a jolt, but my anti-prediction might conceivably help a little. It is, after all, rather distressing to think that the past, including the works of wisdom and beauty which we are wont to admire, may truly be a poor prologue. Only if we sincerely consider our accumulated wisdom as a dubious guide for today and tomorrow can we hope for a fresh start in our thinking. Only then are we free to conceive of a school system free of all the traditions of what schooling is that tend to limit our concept of what schooling can be.

The question remains, however: how can an educational philosophy or program be based on an anti-prediction?

Here, the recent thinking of the Educational Policies Commission is relevant. In its 33-year lifetime, the Commission had a full-time staff with only one mission—to think out basic problems of educational philosophy and policy. The staff, on which I was privileged to serve for ten years, worked without the pressure of deadlines to meet, or of constituencies, other than the twenty Commission members, to satisfy. The publications of the Commission which are pertinent to the present discussion are The Central Purpose of American Education (1961) and Education and The Spirit of Science (1966).*

The Central Purpose of American Education and Education and The Spirit of Science are, in essence, readings of the future out of current trends. They are efforts to reintegrate life, to make sense out of the swirl of events and phenomena that is the modern world. They help us, not to see tomorrow clearly, but to define some of the personal charac-

---

* Both publications are by the Educational Policies Commission of the National Education Association and American Association of School Administrators, Washington, D. C.

teristics that are likely to be of greater value as time passes. I shall now summarize parts of the two EPC statements, taking the liberty of adding some of my subsequent thinking.

Man is in the throes of several revolutions so deep that they render obsolete some of the fundamental attitudes which have guided him throughout history.

He can produce so much in agriculture and in industry that his problem is to make use of all he produces rather than to produce enough to go around. He has so far demonstrated this productivity only here and there, but on a large enough scale to challenge the traditional view that the overwhelming majority of men must live and die on the brink of subsistence.

Man is creating mechanisms which obviate the need for physical labor. He thereby shakes the view that the overwhelming majority of men must spend most of their lives at physical drudgery.

Man has made profound progress in medicine. He is dooming the ancient attitudes that physical pain is a necessary part of life; that mothers and infants must commonly die in childbirth; that any given disease must result in death; and that the earth has enough room to fit all human beings.

Man may verge on the ability to tinker with his genes, subjecting human evolution to his will rather than being subjected to it.

Man has made a quantum leap in his ability to destroy. He can no longer be certain that mankind—or even the United States—will survive, or that human life, when it ends, will be ended by factors beyond human control.

Man is beginning to venture into space. He begins to discern the day when he will no longer consider himself solely, or maybe even primarily, an earthling.

The time needed for communication and transportation between points on earth either has become or is becoming negligible. Our parochialisms—of language, allegiance, habit, and belief—stem largely from the fact that throughout history men have, by technological necessity, belonged to limited segments of mankind. Today, the view that one's neighborhood is but a small part of the earth is losing its validity, and most of the parochialisms which distinguish our cultures from each other have lost their original reason for being.

Man has progressed rapidly in recent years in his ability to ask and answer questions about himself and the world. He is aware of a new ability to predict, to understand, and to control. He also has a heightened perception of his ignorance.

Finally, men everywhere have begun to insist on equality. New countries have formed as once-colonized peoples have insisted on equality among the nations. In the United States, Negroes demand equality of opportunity, thus threatening to destroy a major if shameful facet of the American way of life. So perishes the age-old view that some peoples or races or classes will rule over others.

Any one of these changes, occurring separately, could have shaken human society to the core. Today they are engulfing mankind all at once.

But our analysis is still deficient. The mere listing of changes describes, but fails to explain, what is happening to mankind. If we are to make sense out of the modern world, we must know what caused the various revolutions.

The causes are not far to seek: they are science and technology. In the case of advances in productivity or transportation, this is obvious. As for the questions man asks and the answers he gives, the most striking and productive changes have occurred, not in religion or the humanities or the arts, but in science, with a constant assist from—and to—technology.

The only revolution which does not obviously relate to science and technology is the demand for equality. Yet the relationship, to a considerable extent, is causal.

The Japanese, yellow-skinned as they are, had the bad taste to administer a thrashing to Russians in 1904 and to an assortment of the world's most powerful white nations in the early 1940's. What they needed, to best the white man, was the white man's weapon—advanced technology. The lesson was not lost on colored peoples throughout the world: white men were not automatically dominant. Moreover, in two world wars non-white peoples did much of the fighting for white nations. In doing so, they not only sensed their own worth, but they came into contact

137

with technology and learned to use and appreciate it. They also learned how other nations lived.

In white nations as well as non-white, the masses had for centuries seen that the elite lived well; but now, for the first time, they could raise their expectations because technological progress gave them reason to believe that higher expectations could be satisfied.

Finally, a bit of technology dropped into a culture is like a pebble dropped into a pond. The radio needs repairs, and the factory needs educated or skilled people to operate it. People with new needs or new abilities develop new ideas, and the ripples spread. Some of the people in the society must learn the principles on which their new technology and further technological progress are based, and some must acquire the ability to develop new principles. That is, there must be scientists as well as technicians, or the people will be condemned permanently to lack of understanding and to borrowing from others; and as expectations rise, ignorance and intellectual inferiority become intolerable. Today, virtually every people or its leadership wants respect, health, a higher living standard, and the ability to maintain its national independence. Virtually all of them see scientific and technological development as the keys to those ends. Traditionalist as some of them are, they intentionally drop the pebble into the pond. Soon, more and more people undergo or demand change.

Thus, the great revolutions of the modern world can be traced to science and technology. But these two causes themselves reflect a deeper force—the basic force which is changing our world. In considering that force, we come a little closer to understanding today's world and glimpsing tomorrow's.

It is not a new force, but the extent of its application today is radically new. The Central Purpose of American Education summarizes it in the term "use of the rational powers." The rational powers are listed as the ability to recall and imagine, classify and generalize, compare and evaluate, analyze and synthesize, and deduce and infer. The list hardly makes exciting reading, unless we bear in mind what these abstractions have wrought in the world. The publication derives its title from the contention that development of the rational powers—the movers of the modern age—should be the central purpose of the schools.

If The Central Purpose of American Education enumerates the processes through which the rational powers operate, Education and The Spirit of Science spells out the basic values or preferences that underlie use of the rational powers. These values are: *

1. Longing to know and to understand
2. Questioning of all things
3. Search for data and their meaning
4. Demand for verification
5. Respect for logic
6. Consideration of premises
7. Consideration of consequences

* See National Education Association and American Association of School Administrators, Educational Policies Commission, *Education and the Spirit of Science*. Washington, D. C.: The Commission, 1966. p. 15.

139

These, says the Commission, are the values that underlie science. They are the spirit of science. All forms of scholarship share these values, but it is science that has irresistibly demonstrated their effectiveness, and it is on the wings of science that they have spread around the world.

Actually, science can progress, to an extent, without considering the potential social, or even scientific, consequences of its discoveries. Indeed, there can be a conflict in any field of scholarship between the growth of knowledge and the consideration of consequences, for the growth of knowledge demands that the facts lead where they may. The seventh value, therefore, is not necessarily vital to the so-called pure sciences as practiced. But it is inherent in the spirit of science, which demands maximum awareness and shuns all avoidable ignorance.

Both the rational processes and the values of the spirit of science, as listed here, are clear enough to be pursued as goals of the schools. And they should be pursued by the schools, for:

1. The rational powers, or the spirit of science, have demonstrated their ability—when widely applied to the productive forces in a country— to improve living standards and health and to give men the leisure for education and for other pursuits of their own choosing.

2. The rational powers provide perhaps the best weapons at man's disposal for solving most major problems, including those created or aggravated by use of the rational powers. For

instance, it is probable that the threats of mass destruction and overpopulation, or the problems of urbanization and alienation, can best be attacked not by preaching, praying, or wishing, but by scientific study of man and society. The horrid weapons which science has produced, perhaps more than any other single factor, have aroused suspicion of rationality. But, to paraphrase Charles Frankel's The Case for Modern Man (New York: Harper, 1956), we must not let the dangers of the modern age scare us out of our wits, for they are the only wits we have.

3. The rational powers give men an ever deeper understanding of the world and appreciation of its mysteries. They have brought us such moving and enlightening modern concepts as the invisible border between matter and energy or between life and nonlife. Man has recourse to his rational powers, as he has recourse to religion, because he believes that they lead him to understanding, meaning, and a closer relationship with the universe.

4. The questioning spirit is a strong antidote to fanaticism and arrogance as well as to the acceptance of demagogic leadership. As John Dewey stressed, democratic and scientific thought are closely related.

5. The spread of the spirit of science would give powerful impetus to individuality in the world. Science and technology are often accused of

promoting abject conformity. Certainly, they bear primary responsibility for the growing similarity of cultures. But cultures are precisely groups in which the members are alike in certain ways. Cultures do not individualize us; rather they cause us to act and think like many other people. In some ways technology is doing the same on a worldwide scale as culture does on a smaller scale. However, whatever the impact of science and technology on the differences between groups, the spirit of science multiplies the ability of individuals to be individual. When a person learns to be aware of the influences that play upon him, when he develops the need to understand what he does and why, he increases his ability to be what he wishes to be. He can, for the first time, hope to be an individual. That is what the spirit of science is all about.

6. The spirit of science may be creating the conditions for a genuine community of man. As peoples accept the fruits of technology and, still more, as they develop a scientific and technological capacity of their own, they gradually imbibe the values that underlie science. For this reason, seven values are gradually spreading throughout the world. As the values common to all men increase, the parochialisms which divide men become lesser parts of cultures. These are not minor values; they con-

stitute an approach to life. Beneath the head-lines of dissension that dismay us daily, a foundation of commonality among men may be taking shape. The nation states, which today guarantee our vulnerability to instant death as much as they guarantee our safety,* will not automatically or inevitably crumble before a mankind increasingly united in its way of looking at reality. But the foundation which makes political unity feasible—a sense of one-ness among men—is becoming a little more solid with each passing day.

Religion, based on love of God and man, and conquerors, pitting brute force against human feelings, have sought unity. They have brought some unity, some brotherhood, and much intolerance, hatred, and bloodshed. Science, based on love of knowledge and the power of the mind, may be doing better.

---

* "In the face of an all-out, massive, sophisticated nuclear attack on our cities by a well-designed force, . . . we do not have—nor does it appear feasible to have—a damage-limiting capability which would pre-serve the U. S. as a modern industrial society." Former Air Force Secretary Harold Brown, quoted in *Space Business Daily*, Feb. 28, 1968, p. 324.

IN PRAISE OF PUBLIC SCHOOLS

Consequently, I have reached the point of advocating that the schools develop in young people such unimpeachable traits as a longing for knowledge and a demand for verification. These are hardly original objectives. Though the wording may be different, the ingredients of the spirit of science are among the commonly stated goals of American education.

Yet how many people do we know—high school or college graduates or beyond—who are driven by a deep longing for knowledge? How many who insist on adequate evidence before making up their minds? How many who try to be aware of the assumptions upon which they base their actions and beliefs? Most of us would probably not ascribe these virtues to many people—perhaps not even to ourselves.

Why do the schools so often fail to achieve some of the main goals they claim to pursue?

Before investigating the reasons, let me make it clear that I intend no total condemnation of Ameri-

144

can public education. The schools have served the nation—or at least most of the white majority of the nation—well. If people of diverse background have become one people, it is in large measure because the common school has brought them—or at least most of the white majority—together. Some may lament the diversity which has disappeared in the melting pot; but since Americans, like most people, appear to tolerate diversity poorly, the melting pot may deserve credit for much of the nation's stability. Most of the white majority share in the highest standard of living and the greatest productive capacity of any people in history; in these successes, and in America's vast contributions to world science and culture, the role of the school has been great.

Further to the credit of American educators is the extent to which they recognize a need to change. Change, or else dissatisfaction with the current state of things, is widespread. Both the change and the dissatisfaction are often guided by admirable assumptions:

—that no child is typical of a given age or a given grade;

—that children learn best when they learn at their own pace and when each learning experience is appropriate to each child;

—that all pupils, and not just the white middle class, should be able to profit from public education;

—that schools have too commonly impaired the curiosity and individuality of children;

—that learning improves when pupils are given latitude for initiative rather than being passive recipients of education;

—that knowledge is often too compartmentalized in the schools;

—that education should profit from technological progress;

—that the time of teachers is not used as efficiently as it could be;

—that the content of education should be abreast of the latest knowledge;

—that students should seek and discover answers rather than memorize them;

—that it is more important to learn the principles and concepts of a discipline than to learn the mere facts.

These assumptions, combined with the openness of American schools to public evaluation, are keeping the best of our schools in a healthy ferment.

Thus, some schools have switched, most commonly in the primary years, to a nongraded program. Pupils progress at their own best pace, without the shackles of promotion and failure to lock them into steps of predetermined length. In other cases, schools recognize individual differences through multi-grading, in which each pupil may be in different grades for different subjects.

Some schools today give pupils broad scope for independent study during part of the school day. These programs are usually limited to talented pupils and to the last two years of high school. The students may have periods of some school time without assigned classes. They may carry out, under only general supervision, long-term assignments worked out between the teacher and the individual pupil. They may, on their own initiative, use any of the school's resources for work as individuals or in groups. In some cases, high school students are not required to attend classes, or may leave class at any time.

Some schools vary class size or length of period according to the purpose of the group or permit teachers to schedule their meetings with pupils in whatever manner seems most appropriate to their objectives.

Other frontiers of education today are in the fields of electronics and, despite widespread disenchantment with currently available materials, programmed learning. Advances in these fields may eventually permit every pupil to have immediate access to any item of stored knowledge anywhere in the country at the push of a button, or to progress through each subject at his own rate. The day is approaching, too, when computers and programs will be widely used not only to teach knowledge and basic or vocational skills, but also to develop more sophisticated abilities—such as those of interpretation, analysis, synthesis, and extrapolation.

A major effort in curriculum reform, particularly since Sputnik in October 1957, has been to improve the courses themselves in several ways—by bringing their content up to date, by emphasizing principles rather than facts, and by stressing the recognition and solution of problems rather than the learning of pat answers. Researchers have labored with school teachers to produce new textbooks and courses of this sort in a variety of subjects. Joint development of courses is becoming a tradition, and its products have gained wide popularity. Indeed, the new chemistry, math, and physics are among the most common innovations of the high school curriculum today.

While many schools are trying to improve the teaching of individual subjects, others are moving to blur the traditional boundaries between subjects. For example, many schools have recently introduced humanities courses, in which a team of teachers tries to integrate history, literature, drama, band, music, art, and philosophy.

Other innovations are: team teaching; use of teacher aides; a broadened role for teachers in school-policy making; the subordination of textbooks to other learning resources; new types of school buildings; foreign-language teaching by new methods and at lower age levels; extension of universal public education downward to age four and upward to the second year beyond the high school; increased attention to public relations between school and community; and the granting of permission to some teachers of disadvantaged children to develop their own curriculums and choose their own materials.

In short, the accomplishments of American public education are vast, and many educators are struggling honorably to keep the schools abreast of new challenges.

BUT . . .

*By 2020 we will realize "that solving an elegant mathe-
matical problem and making love are only different classes
in the same order of things, sharing common ecstasy."—
George B. Leonard and John Poppy of* Look *Magazine,
at meeting of American Institute of Planners, October 1967.*

Whatever their past accomplishments and present
efforts, the schools have often achieved what could
diplomatically be termed less than the desired impact. In particular, they infrequently turn out graduates imbued for a lifetime with any part of the spirit
of science. Why?

The failures are partly due to underfinancing and
overcrowding. These culprits are constantly and quite
justifiably blamed for educational failures, minor and
major. But in the case of sophisticated goals, like
those embodied in the spirit of science, I believe
that the schools would generally fail even if teachers
were paid like doctors and even if classes were

smaller. The schools would fail even if disadvantaged ghetto pupils disappeared or became middle class like the rest of us, willing and able to do what the teacher says.

They would continue to fail in part because of . . . madness. Our society is afraid of some characteristics which it admires. For example, we consider it virtuous to come to one's own conclusions—provided the conclusions are fairly conventional. The schools have faithfully reflected American schizophrenia on such matters. They have had to regard thinking—the essence of the spirit of science—as potentially subversive, particularly in such crucial fields as sex, religion, and politics. Therefore, they have been inadequately devoted to the spirit of science.

But the main reason for inadequate devotion to the spirit of science is devotion to subjects. In theory, the two devotions need not be contradictory, but in practice they are.

Teachers often state that the subjects they teach are merely means to deeper ends. History, for example, is purportedly intended less to give a knowledge of Columbus than to heighten the pupils' understanding of the present, their sense of responsibility, or their ability to think. Similarly, it is claimed that literature will make pupils receptive to beauty, better rounded, and more humane. Chemistry, it is claimed, will give them greater understanding of the world and make them more rational in their daily lives.

Unfortunately, however resounding the advertised virtues of a subject, it is the content that tends to be emphasized when it is taught. It is to the content that pupils try valiantly to wed themselves—at least, until exams do them part. In educators, the subject-matter mania manifests itself in worship of such subject-centered gods as articulation and balance.

Educators regard as obvious a need to have the learning of one year follow from, and build upon, that of the previous year. Courses are planned in which intermediate learning of mathematics assumes certain elementary knowledge of mathematics. History courses are planned in which the pupil who studies Reconstruction has earlier learned about the Civil War. There may be lively disagreement in defining the needed prerequisites or the logical follow-up in any given case, but curriculums tend to be planned on the assumption that one thing must follow another.

This assumption seems logically impeccable. But its fruits are psychologically abhorrent. The controlling consideration in what happens to Jimmy is not the free pursuit of, or even the effort to find out, what may most benefit him at a given moment, but the demands of the subject.

Another object of adulation is balance in the curriculum. Educators and other citizens complain that certain subjects are overemphasized and others underemphasized. They may contend that there is too much science and too little art in the curriculum, or that non-Western history is neglected.

Why this obsession with subjects? Why do teachers either permit the content to crowd out the deeper ends or relegate the accomplishment of those ends to an assumed automatic spin-off from the learning of the content?

Subjects typically become ends in themselves for several reasons.

First: subjects are what teachers know best how to teach; they know better how to produce knowledge of facts or concepts than questioning of facts or concepts.

Second: teachers tend to teach as they were taught. When today's teachers were school children, it was usually obvious to them that courses in various subjects were intended above all to teach those subjects.

Third: today also teachers and pupils both know that they will in practice be judged largely on the basis of subject-matter accomplishments. They will be so judged regardless of the pompous statements of purpose issued by schools, school boards, and policies commissions. A good memory is the most effective weapon for gaining admission to the college of one's choice. Tests of the higher mental abilities are being improved, but facts, concepts, and basic skills are the overwhelmingly usual objects for tests to measure. Pupils and classes are generally rated not by their ability to think or create, but by their accumulation of knowledge.

Thus, a teacher whose pupils are actually developing into exceptionally thoughtful citizens may be rated a failure if his class does not "know" enough history. A comparison of two hypothetical physics classes will lead to a similar conclusion. In one, the pupils learn a considerable amount of physics; in the other, the pupils develop so deep a regard for the scientific principles of uncertainty and demand for evidence that they begin to apply these principles in other facets of their lives. Almost invariably, the teacher of the former class will reap the rewards of recognition as a good physics teacher, unless the pupils of the second class happen to do as well or better on subject-matter tests given by the school or by college admissions authorities.

Common sense, if nothing else, tells most teachers that the way to teach a subject is to cover it! It takes a foolhardy teacher to keep his eyes steadfastly on the deeper purposes of education.

In 1902, in The Child and the Curriculum, John Dewey lamented the effects of confronting pupils with facts "torn away from their original place in experience and rearranged with reference to some general principle." Curriculums, he found, succeeded ingeniously in converting the wonder of learning into "an external annex to the child's present life." Two-thirds of a century later, how many schools continue to make learning a punishment and to create a situation in which only dictatorial methods will elicit work from pupils?

A PLEA FOR IGNORANCE?

"When we were boys, boys had to do a little work in school. They were not coaxed; they were hammered. Spelling, writing, and arithmetic were not electives; and you had to learn.

"In these more fortunate times, elementary education has become in many places a sort of vaudeville show. The child must be kept amused and learns what he pleases. Many sage teachers scorn the old-fashioned rudiments, and it seems to be regarded as between misfortune and a crime for a child to learn to read."—New York Sun *editorial, 1902. Quoted in* Phi Delta Kappan, *October 1958, p. 42.*

Perhaps it is far-fetched to speak of dictatorial methods and American schools in the same breath. Just because daily attendance is required by law . . . just because a pupil is subjected to rules and demands that are largely not of his own making . . . just because he has a choice between pleasing the authorities and being in trouble the rest of his life . . . just because the entire atmosphere tells him that he needs to be told what is good for him, that his own initiatives and drives would be a miserable basis for his own best development, and that his salvation is benevolently assured through an installment plan prepared by his wiser elders—are these adequate reasons for juxtaposing education and dictatorship?

Perhaps an apology is in order. But some readers may divine in the preceding section other follies beyond expiation. If I oppose subjects, what do I favor? Ignorance? Am I one of those ludicrous progressive educators who intend to produce people who think they can think, but who know nothing? Don't I believe there is some knowledge which everyone needs if he is to live fruitfully? Doesn't everyone need some American history, mathematics, biology, English literature? Can I expect a teacher to teach any subject that may come up, rather than require pupils to focus their attention on the subject he knows best?

The truth is that I am categorically opposed to ignorance. As for the other questions, they suggest further questions in rebuttal: Is the ability to think or criticize in danger of being developed without recourse to content? If useful knowledge or skills are to be acquired, must courses or units be planned to teach them? Is the best progress of a student, or even his maximum acquisition of knowledge, fostered by requiring him at a certain time each day to dedicate himself, alone or with a class, to something so specific as the learning of a given subject, a given group of subjects, or a given concept? Must we fight the Battle of the Mold with every student who comes our way?

Admittedly, these questions are not satisfactory answers. But one must ponder them in order to understand why giving pupils a virtually limitless range of individual choice enhances learning and is compatible with orderly, efficient school administration.

Most teachers, hopefully, would reject the allegation that their work consists of forcing pupils into a mold. Yet, whatever the subject or skill he is teaching, a teacher must try to make (or, to use a kinder euphemism, to help) all his pupils learn a certain amount of the subject or concept by a certain deadline. Skillful teachers will arouse each pupil's interest in the work and will permit and encourage each pupil to move ahead at his own pace. But, considering the other possibilities for learning at that moment, this is really a minor concession to individual differences and a still smaller concession to individual dignity; skillful teachers merely render the mold a little more flexible.

Most education in the United States, and still more in many other countries, consists of pools ladled out of the ocean of knowledge, with each pupil required to swim a lap each year. Some schools are flexible enough to let pupils swim two laps if they can, or not to disgrace those pupils who can cover only half a lap. Or perhaps a school is an assembly line on which more or less the same components of knowledge and skill are applied to

156

each passerby. As Quentin Brew, an educational psychologist in New Zealand, has put it, most educators would announce the millenium if a pill to increase memory one-hundred-fold became available.

What does this sort of education do for (or to) people? It gives them the ability to read and write. It gives them some knowledge which remains with them for a considerable time. It helps to make them respectable contributors to the nation's economic well-being. It may stimulate a life-long interest in some field.

These are no mean accomplishments. But certainly there is another side of the ledger, too. How many of us have learned in school to dislike one or more subjects, or even all learning, even if we started school with the wide-ranging curiosity of a child? How much of what we did in school produced no long-range impact of any sort, favorable or unfavorable? To be blunter, how much of our time was just plain wasted? On command, we learned to read. How many of us like to read today? On command, we studied a few classics of English literature. How many of us ever return to the classics? On command, we learned some science. How many of us have the foggiest notion of the make-up of the synthetics we wear or about any other scientific matter that is vital in our daily lives? More important, how many of us are motivated to combat our ignorance?

How many students, stemming from a background ill-fitted to the required mold, have learned in school to scorn themselves? How many times have schools teamed up with families and communities to destroy a child or to consolidate his destruction? How many pupils have quit school to escape from the horrors of self-contempt?

The dropout is an obvious loss to himself and to society, particularly if he becomes a public charge or a law-breaker. Yet the apparently successful student may represent almost as great a waste of potential. How developed is the mind of a man whose basic learning experience has consisted of doing what he is told? Should we rejoice when a pupil consistently achieves high grades, thereby demonstrating perhaps nothing more substantial than an excellent adjustment to an arbitrary, artificial, and repressive environment?

Education is generally so rigid that what is surprising is not the extent of its failure but the extent of its success. Could there be a greater tribute to the adaptability of the young? Imagine what the outcome would be if most pupils were as inflexible as the expectations of most schools!

The knowledge explosion gives hope. It may eventually overwhelm those who suffer from a compulsion to plan curriculum. They may lose faith in their assumed ability to shrink the world's knowledge down to manageable size. The schools, set adrift in a turbulent ocean, will no longer be able to ladle out a tidy pool of knowledge and to define their activities in terms of subject matter. They will be free, at last, to pursue the goals they always claimed to be pursuing anyway—and their pupils will learn more subject-matter than ever before.

THE REST OF THE POEM

"I don't understand," came the young girl's reply.
"My love," said the father, "Let's try, you and I,
to imagine a world of women and men
who are deep and wise thinkers. It could be that
 then
the ills caused by people would soon disappear,
and good would be done out of thought, not
 from fear.
Wasted time, prejudice, drugs, too much drink,
All crave blind emotion and flee minds that think.
The fanatic made gentle, his certainty blurring,
The oppressor made conscious, the sleeper now
 stirring.
And justice's cries would so gladly be heeded
That recourse to violence wouldn't be needed.
For to stand idly by when a man is enslaved
would be deemed by us all to be deeply depraved.
And all men on earth, if they're willing to hear it,
all would be freed, by the questioning spirit,
from the bonds of their birth and the chains of
 their cultures,
from the unchallenged learnings that make people
 vultures.
Our brief link to eternity, so often wasted,
if we questioned all things could more fully be tasted.
How should life be? Well, perhaps we can try
to answer it this way: The good life is 'Why?' "

The End